A RESOURCE BOOK FOR CHILDREN'S GROUPS AND ASSEMBLIES

Alan Procter

a Many Rooms publication

*Dedicated to all the pupils who have listened patiently
to my talks, and to three headmasters
who have given me unfailing support and encouragement;
Peter Wright (Caldicott), Mike Spens (Caldicott)
and Innes MacAskill (Beeston Hall).*

My thanks go to Mrs Viv Farnell who typed out the original manuscript, and coped so efficiently with my terrible handwriting, and to Michael Freeland for his wise advice.

Contents

Contents continued

Martin Luther King
15 January

Martin Luther King was the son of a Baptist minister. As a boy,
he wished to be a doctor but changed his mind and became a Baptist
minister like his father.

Racial discrimination, judging people as inferior because of the
colour of their skin, was rife in the United States. When Martin Luther
King was pastor of Dexter Avenue Baptist Church in Montgomery,
Alabama, a crisis arose. On 1st December, 1955, a black woman was
arrested for not giving up her seat to a white person on a bus. Martin
argued for a peaceful solution, a boycott of the buses. His voice was
heard and obeyed and the boycott went on for over a year.

On 21st December 1956, the United States Supreme Court ruled
that segregation on buses was wrong. That ruling was just the
beginning. The Civil Rights movement grew in strength and influence,
though keeping the strategy of non-violence. It adopted the old
cotton-workers' hymn 'We Shall Overcome' as its anthem in its efforts
to overcome prejudice and hatred.

On 28th August, 1963, two hundred thousand people marched to
the Lincoln Memorial in Washington to campaign for civil rights.
Martin Luther King delivered his greatest speech which included the
words: "I have a dream... It is a dream deeply rooted in the American
dream ... a dream that my four little children will one day live in a
nation where they will not be judged by the colour of their skin but by
the content of their character."

As a leader of the Southern Christian Leadership Conference he
helped to bring about the Civil Rights Act (1964) and the Voting
Rights Act (1965). It was his leadership that inspired a non-violent
policy. He based his philosophy on the teachings of Jesus and also
Gandhi.

Martin said, "We will match your capacity to inflict suffering with
our capacity to endure suffering.... We will not hate you, but we
cannot ... obey your unjust laws.... We will so appeal to your heart and

conscience that we will win you over in the process."

In 1964 Martin was awarded the Nobel Peace Prize. He gave the substantial prize money away to Civil Rights organisations because he regarded the prize as a recognition of everyone's efforts, not just his own. He was loved and respected by millions, but also hated and treated as a trouble maker. He had been arrested often, once stabbed, once stoned and his house had been bombed. On 4th April, 1968, the day before a mass march, he was shot and killed by an assassin, on a hotel balcony in Memphis, Tennessee. He is buried on a small hillside in Atlanta.

Thought

In Christ Jesus, there is no longer division; there is no Jew or Greek, no slave or free, no longer male and female. In Christ Jesus, we are all one. The risen Christ is not confined by the walls of hatred and suspicion, of injustice and fear. In Christ is our freedom and our hope.

Prayer

Creator God, you created all men and women equal in your sight. You invite us to live in harmony and peace with each other and with you. Where we have built walls to divide us from our neighbour, call us back to the unity for which you made us. In Christ Jesus, draw us together, that our broken world might be made whole. We ask this through the same Christ Jesus our Lord, who lives and reigns with you and the Holy Spirit, one God for ever and ever. Amen.

God who made us, love us.
God who loves us, forgive us.
God who forgives us, heal us.
God who heals us, unite us.
God who unites us, grant us peace.

Edward Lear
29 January

Although it is well over a hundred years old, 'The Owl and the Pussycat' was top of the list of children's favourite poems in 2001. The man who composed it made his living writing nonsense.

Edward Lear was born on 12th May 1812 at Highgate, near London. He was the youngest of 21 children. His mother died and he was brought up by his eldest sister, Ann. Edward had a great talent for drawing and from the age of fifteen earned his living in this way. In 1831 he was employed by the Zoological Society of London and specialised in drawing birds, especially parrots. Later he worked for the British Museum and after that for the Earl of Derby. It was whilst he was sketching the Earl's private collection of animals that he was introduced to the Earl's grandchildren. It was for them that he produced a 'Book of Nonsense'. Weak eyesight made him turn from detailed work to landscape paintings. In 1846 he gave drawing lessons to Queen Victoria.

Lear's health was never good, he suffered from epilepsy, and so he left Britain for a better climate. He was a brilliant letter writer, illustrating his writings with humorous sketches. He died on 29th January 1888, at San Remo, in Italy.

Edward Lear is remembered for his nonsense poetry, The Akond of Swat, The Jumblies, 'The Owl and the Pussycat', The Pobble who had no toes and his 'Self-Portrait of the Laureate of Nonsense'.

How pleasant to know Mr Lear!
Who has written such volumes of stuff!
Some think him ill-tempered and queer,
But a few think him pleasant enough.
His mind is concrete and fastidious,
His nose is remarkably big;
His visage is more or less hideous,
His beard it resembles a wig.

He has ears, and two eyes, and ten fingers,
Leastways, if you reckon two thumbs;
Long ago he was one of the singers,
But now he is one of the dumbs.

He sits in a beautiful parlour,
With hundreds of books on the wall;
He drinks a great deal of Marsala,
But never gets tipsy at all.

He has many friends, laymen and clerical;
Old Foss is the name of his car;
His body is perfectly spherical,
He weareth a runcible hat.

When he walks in a waterproof white,
The children run after him so!
Calling out, 'He's come out in his night-
Gown, that crazy old Englishman, oh!'

He weeps by the side of the ocean,
He weeps on the top of the hill;
He purchases pancakes and lotion,
And chocolate shrimps from the mill.

He reads but he cannot speak Spanish,
He cannot abide ginger-beer:
Ere the days of his pilgrimage vanish,
How pleasant to know Mr Lear!

He also made the limerick popular.
Here is one of his examples:
There was an old Man who said, "How
Shall I flee from this horrible cow?

I will sit on this stile,
And continue to smile,
Which may soften the heart of that cow."

You might like to have a go at writing your own.

Thought

Joy is a gift from God, and laughter comes from a joyful heart. To laugh purely and simply is to give praise to God. Laughter can overcome fear, unite people and heal. There is indeed a time for everything: weeping, laughing, mourning and dancing. Rejoice, laugh, clap your hands give praise to God!

Prayer

God of joy, you give us your Holy Spirit that we might rejoice and be glad in your presence. You lighten our days with laughter, and put a song of praise on our lips. Fill us again with your joy; let us share it with others that sadness and despair may be banished, and every tear wiped away. We ask this through Jesus Christ, your well-loved Son, in whom you rejoice with the Holy Spirit for ever. Amen.

Grant us your peace, O Lord
that your peace might help us rejoice.
May our rejoicing brighten each day
and laughter fill our homes
so all peoples will know that you are our God.

St Valentine
14 February

Pope Gelasius appointed an official feast of St Valentine in the year of 494 and later named St Valentine as the patron saint of lovers.

There seem to have been two Valentines who were martyrs. One was a Roman priest and physician who was killed during the persecution of the Emperor Claudius II. Whilst in prison Valentine converted the Roman officer Asterius, to whose care he was committed, together with his wife and family. The Emperor had Valentine beaten with rods, and beheaded on 14th February 270. He was buried on the Via Flaminia, where a church was afterwards built by Pope Julius I. The second Valentine was the Bishop of Terni, who was martyred in Rome, but his relics were returned to Terni. It is possible that both accounts may refer to the same man. A story says that Valentine, having cured her of blindness, fell in love with Asterius' daughter, and that he left a little love note behind for her when he was taken out to be killed. He had signed it, 'Your Valentine'.

Perhaps this story of true love was the Church's answer to the Roman feast of Lupercalia, which was celebrated on 15th February. This feast was connected with fertility. The Lupercal was a cave where, by tradition, the she-wolf acted as foster-mother to Romulus and Remus, the founders of Rome. After various animal sacrifices and ceremonies, young men ran through the crowd carrying strips of dog skin and had to hit the women in the crowd. This was said to promote fertility, so women who wanted children stood close to the race. The strips of skin were called 'februa' (that which purifies). Our month name February comes from the same word. This 'feast of the wolf' may have some connection with the expression 'wolf whistle'.

It is said that on 14th February, birds choose their mates. It was traditional that the first unmarried man a young lady met on St Valentine's Day would become her sweetheart and would marry her. Oliver Cromwell abolished St Valentine's Day but when the monarchy was restored so was the feast. As time went on gifts were sent with the messages; often these gifts were small and personal, stockings, ribbons, garters or gloves. With gloves, a suitable message might be:

Go, little gloves, salute my own dear Valentine
Who was, who is, who must, who shall be mine.
My love, to you I send these gloves.
If you love me, leave out the 'g',
And make a pair of loves.

In the nineteenth century St Valentine's Day was the busiest day of the year for postmen. When the Christmas card became popular, sending Valentines decreased dramatically. There has been something of a commercial comeback in the last thirty years.

Perhaps it is not all commercialism. There should always be times when we say 'I love you', certainly more often than once a year. A little more romance, a little less selfishness, a little more consideration for others, that is what St Valentine's Day is all about. Valentine cards could be home-made, to show how much you love someone. Today is a day to show real love, not sentimentality but real love, care and thought for those who are the most precious to us in this world.

Thought

Love cannot be bought or sold, it cannot be commanded or controlled. Love is fragile, but love endures, even beyond death. God is love, so wherever love is, God is there; and wherever God is, love is there. Living in love is living in God, and living in God is loving in God.

Prayer

You made us, God, to love us, and when we love you, we are truly alive. Help us to appreciate your love, that we might have grateful hearts; and knowing how much you love us, we might want to love others in the same way. Let us show our love for each other by being kind, generous and honest, forgiving each other and helping each other. In this way, we become more and more like you, whose nature is love. And bring us one day to heaven, where we will live in perfect love for ever. We ask this through Jesus Christ, who shows us your love. Amen.

In the morning, love us O Lord.
In the daytime, love us O Lord.
In the afternoon, love us O Lord.
In the evening, love us O Lord.
When darkness falls, love us O Lord.
All through the night, love us O Lord .

Shrove Tuesday

The Anglo-Saxon verb 'scrifan' meant 'to impose a penance', usually prayers to be said for sins committed. The past tense of the verb was 'shrove', which is how this day gets its name.

It was the day when people went to church to confess their sins, do penance, and receive absolution. If you are a Roman Catholic then you may well continue this custom. The Sunday, Monday, and Tuesday before Ash Wednesday are known as Shrovetide. The Sunday is called Quinquagesima – 'fifty days' to Easter, and the Monday 'Collop Monday', when slices of meat or bacon were eaten. Meat was forbidden in Lent, so the housewives fried their escalopes so that all the meat was eaten. Eggs, cream, fat and butter were also forbidden during Lent, so these were mixed with flour and milk and made into pancakes that were eaten on Shrove Tuesday. The sticky dough was cooked slowly over a fire and tossed occasionally to stop it burning. Hence the custom of eating pancakes on Shrove Tuesday.

In the past Shrove Tuesday was a holiday. Children had a day off school and the universities were shut. This gave a great opportunity for merry-making; in particular it gave time for football and other games. At Ashbourne in Derbyshire 'Uptown' plays 'Downtown' (which side you are in depends on where you were born in the town). The game is a cross between football and rugby and can be very violent. The goals are two mill-stones, three miles apart. A famous pancake race is held at Olney in Buckinghamshire. The race dates back to 1445 when a housewife heard the church bell calling her to the service. She rushed out of her house wearing her apron, and carrying her pancake with her. Women over eighteen years of age, who have lived in Olney for at least 3 months may take part in the race today. Wearing an apron, and carrying a pancake, which has to be tossed three times, the woman must run about a quarter of a mile from the market square to the church. The winner gets a prayer book from the Vicar, and the runner-up gets a kiss from the Verger.

In French speaking countries today is 'Mardi Gras' or 'Fat Tuesday'; in Germany it is 'Fetter Dienstag'. People revel in a carnival atmosphere.

The word 'Carnival' comes from the Latin 'carnem levare' – to put away flesh. After the merriment of today comes the solemn season of Lent.

Because Easter is a moveable feast, the Last Supper may have been the Passover meal the date of which was determined by a full moon; the dates of Shrove Tuesday and Ash Wednesday are moveable too. Easter Sunday is the Sunday following the first full moon after the Spring Equinox (March 20th). If the full moon occurs on the Sunday then Easter is the Sunday after. Easter Sunday may fall between 22nd March and 25th April; Shrove Tuesday may fall between 3rd February and 9th March.

Thought

Forgiveness is important. When we ask for forgiveness, we are saying that we want to put our wrongdoing behind us and to begin again. The Lord does not want us to live in misery: on the contrary, the Lord wants us to live well and to rejoice. So we turn to the Lord and ask for a spirit of forgiveness, that we might find joy.

Prayer

Lord God, help us to know when to celebrate and when to hold back. Strengthen our will, that we might truly choose good, and be able to live as we choose. When we face temptation, help us to resist, that habits of goodness may be ours. Lead us back when we stray, forgive us when we sin, and guide us when we are confused. We are your people, and you are our God. We ask this through Christ our Lord. Amen.

Let us live the whole year through
Weeping with those who weep
Rejoicing with those who rejoice
and helping those in need.
Make us strong
and keep us yours.
In Jesus Christ. Amen.

Ash Wednesday

Today is the first of the forty days of Lent. Lent actually lasts longer than forty days because Sundays are not fast days, so they are not included in the reckoning. Forty days was the time Moses and Elijah spent in the wilderness in the Old Testament, and Jesus spent in the wilderness, being tempted, in the New Testament. In fact, 'forty days' just means 'a long time', though the Church takes the words literally. The word Lent comes from the Old English word 'lencten', the Spring, when the days begin to lengthen.

Today is Ash Wednesday. In the Old Testament the sign of sorrow was 'sackcloth and ashes'. Rough sackcloth was worn and cold ashes from the fire were sprinkled over the head. (See Esther 4:1-3, as one example.) The sackcloth was sometimes goat or camel hair. Today in many churches there will be a service of 'Imposition of the Ashes'. Palm crosses will have been burnt to ashes and some of the ash will be put on the foreheads of the people present. The priest reminds them that they are mortal and must one day die and give account to God. "Remember, you are but dust, and to dust you shall return". These words are echoed in the funeral service, "Dust to dust, ashes to ashes".

Lent is a period of fasting, which originally meant giving up meat, eggs, fat, and so on. The fourth Sunday in Lent, half way through, was a time of relaxation of these strict rules. It is called Refreshment Sunday. Nowadays it is also called Mothering Sunday, which originally had nothing to do with Mother's Day, (which was started in the U.S.A. in 1906). Mothering Sunday was, originally, the time when everyone went to the mother church of their parish (the main church). In the eighteenth century and nineteenth century servants were allowed to go home on this Sunday, so they would take a present for their mothers, flowers or Simnel cake. Simnel cake is made from currants, peel, spice, and fine flour. The cake may have got its name from the Latin word for flour, 'simila'; another story says that the cake was named after two children, a boy called Simon and a girl called Nellie. Fasting has gradually gone out of fashion, but Roman Catholics often fast on Ash

Wednesday and Good Friday. In the Middle Ages fish replaced meat: every monastery had stew-ponds where fish were kept. In 1562 a person who ate meat on a fast day faced a fine of £3, a lot of money in those days or three months in prison.

Nowadays people try to discipline themselves during Lent. It is a time when we can try to be less selfish and self-centred; we may try to give more time to God by attending extra services, or by making time to reflect and meditate; we may try to help others more. A poem called "To Keep a true Lent" by Robert Herrick follows that theme:

Is this a Fast, to keep
The larder lean?
And clean
From fat of veals and sheep?

Is it to quit the dish
Of flesh, yet still
To fill
The platter high with fish?

Is it to fast an hour
Or ragg'd to go
Or show
A down-cast look and sour?

No; 'tis a Fast to dole
Thy sheaf of wheat
And meat
Unto the hungry soul.

It is to fast from strife
And old debate,
And hate;
To circumcise thy life.

To show a heart grief-rent;
To starve thy sin,
Not bin;
And that's to keep thy Lent.

Thought

What visible sign will show that we are turning back to the Lord? Should we wear badge or cross, hold some token of sin and throw it away? Let us mark ourselves with ash, signifying the end of the old and the beginning of the new. And let the mark of ash be in the shape of a cross, to show that we are returning to Christ. Ash reminds us we will return to the dust from which we came; the cross reminds us we will rise with Christ.

Prayer

Call us back, O Lord, to your ways. Keep us faithful to your will. Remind us of your promise of life. Let us live the sign we wear, of repentance and new life. We know we are weak, but in your strength we can be strong; your strength, though, is gentle, and shows your love. For this, and for all your gifts, we give you thanks. Amen.

You have planted in our heart
a desire to return to you.
You hold out before us
your open, welcoming arms.
Could we resist?
Let us return
and our heart find peace.

St David
1 March

Do you know the patron saints of the British Isles? St George for England, St Andrew for Scotland, St Patrick for Ireland, and St David for Wales. But which saint was the only one to be born in his patronal country? It was St David, who is also called Dewi or Dafydd.

We know very little about David. Most of what we do know was written in the eleventh century, a mixture of history, legend and fable. His father was a prince and his mother, who became a Saint, was Non. David was brought up as a Christian and educated at Henfynw, in Cardigan, where he was said to be 'full of grace and lovely to behold'. Then he became a priest and studied for ten years under Paulinus the Scribe. There is a tale that Paulinus lost his sight after a severe illness. The monks looked into his eyes to try to find out the cause of the blindness, but David would not, because he had never raised his eyes to his master's face. Paulinus praised him for this, but asked David to touch and bless his eyes. His sight was restored.

David became a missionary founding monasteries in Wales and Cornwall and he may even have travelled with St Non to Brittany. David's own monastery was founded in Menevia, when he was thirty years old. After his death the place was known as St David's. His rule was strict: one meal a day of bread, vegetables, eggs, milk and water. David's nickname was "Aquaticus" because his monks were allowed only water, not beer or wine. He believed in heavy manual labour; the monks even had to pull their own ploughs. Silence was encouraged, so the monks spent most of the day without speaking. It is said that David was made archbishop, so he chose to build his cathedral at Menevia. He founded many churches in Wales, and over fifty bear his name. He died at Menevia on 1st March, in either 589 or possibly 601. His last message was, 'Brothers and sisters, be joyful and keep your faith and do the little things that you have seen and heard with me.' Huge crowds visited him to receive his blessing, and when he died they were overcome with grief. It is said 'Kings mourned him as a judge, the older people mourned him as a brother, the younger as a father.'

He was buried in the cathedral-abbey church. Many miracles have been connected with David, including healings and the appearance of wells, like at Ffynnon Feddyg.

St David's became, and still is, a place of pilgrimage. In the Middle Ages two pilgrimages to St David's were equal to one to Rome. (In the early twelfth Century David was canonised at the request of Henry I.)

Both leeks and daffodils are associated with St David. The leek was possibly his emblem. It was worn by Welsh soldiers at Poitiers, because it was supposed to protect the wearer from harm. The Welsh Guards wear leeks on St David's Day. The daffodil is also a welsh emblem. The daffodil comes from 'asphodel' (which is also a yellow flower with pointed leaves). The asphodel was said by poets to be immortal and to grow on the Elysian fields, in Greek mythology where the blessed went after death.

Thought

David was full of grace. He showed in his life clear signs of the presence of the Holy God. To meet him was to meet humility, austerity, dedication and holiness. David was faithful to the Lord, and the Lord blessed him. All who are faithful to the Lord are blessed; all who are faithful to the Lord are full of grace.

Prayer

Lord, your goodness transforms the lives of women and men in every age, showing your wisdom and power. Transform us as you transformed David, that we might be joyful, keep our faith, and do the little things of life well. May your gospel be proclaimed in the way we live and through the words we speak. So may you receive glory, honour and praise, this day and every day. Through Christ our Lord. Amen.

In the morning let us greet you, Lord.
In the daytime, let us thank you,
in the evening let us praise you,
and always let us contemplate your glory,
in Christ Jesus our Lord. Amen.

St Perpetua & companions

7 March

A violent persecution of Christians under the Emperor Septimus Severus began in 202. The Emperor had forbidden new conversions to Christianity, which meant that people learning about Christianity, called catechumens, were liable to arrest and death. The persecution began in Rome and spread through the Empire, reaching Carthage in 203. Perpetua, a young married woman aged twenty-two, was arrested with four others; a pregnant slave Felicitas, her husband Revocatus, and two other men, Saturninus and Secundulus. Perpetua had a baby son, just a few months old.

At first the Christians were kept under guard in a private house. Perpetua's father visited her and begged her to renounce her faith, arguing strongly that the baby would suffer too. All five prisoners remained firm in their faith, and were moved into a prison. Felicitas gave birth to a girl there.

In prison Perpetua experienced several visions. One vision was of a golden ladder reaching from earth to heaven. It was very narrow and had hooks and knives fastened to its sides. At the bottom was a dragon which tried to frighten away people trying to climb the ladder. She saw one of her companions climb first and call her to follow. She did so, and found herself in the presence of a shepherd surrounded by thousands of white-robed companions. This she took to be a warning that she would soon be martyred. Perpetua wrote her visions down and an eye witness finished the story. The martyrs had to wait several days for the death sentence to be carried out; they were to be thrown to wild animals. They left prison for the amphitheatre "joyfully as though they were on their way to heaven".

Animals had been prepared; leopards and bears for the men, a mad heifer for the women. Saturninus was mauled by a leopard. The heifer knocked Perpetua over but she was so absorbed in ecstasy that she seems to have been unaware of what had happened. She only accepted what had happened when shown the marks on her dress and body. The martyrs exchanged a final kiss of peace, and were then stabbed in the throat. Perpetua guided the knife to her throat. The eye-witness wrote, "It was as though so great a woman... could not be despatched unless she herself were willing."

The feast of these martyrs became very famous in the whole Church and is mentioned in the earliest calendars. In 1907 an inscription in their honour was discovered at Carthage in the Basilica Majorum where they were buried. "Bravest and happiest martyrs! You were called and chosen for the glory of our Lord Jesus Christ." (From the account of the martyrdom of the Holy Martyrs of Carthage.)

Thought

Perpetua became a Christian in a time of persecution. She was young, with the whole of her life before her; but she felt that without Christ, her life would be nothing. Rather than renounce him, she willingly embraced death. She has been a constant inspiration for Christians facing persecution.

Prayer

Your way is the way of the Cross, O Lord. Following you, we seek life in all its fullness. To die is for us to enter into eternal life. Help us to value our faith and to grow in faith, that we will understand your love for us more and more each day. As Perpetua and her companions were faithful to you until the end, so may we live and die knowing you are with us always, and knowing you bring us peace. You, who live and reign with the Father and the Holy Spirit, one God for ever and ever. Amen.

Let us live for you, Lord Jesus.
Let us love you, Lord Jesus.
Let us serve you, Lord Jesus.
Let us share your Good News with others.
Let us enjoy heaven for ever.

Kenneth Grahame

8 March

Kenneth Grahame was born in Edinburgh of an old Scottish family. His mother died when he was three years old and, with his two brothers and his sister, he went to live with his grandmother at Cookham Dean in Berkshire. He missed his mother very much and began to make up stories and to daydream. He went to school in Oxford but did not go to university because money was scarce. In 1879 he became a clerk in the Bank of England; he worked hard and was Secretary of the Bank from 1898-1907.

It was not the sort of life he wanted; he disliked the city and dreamed of the countryside. He wrote sketches, essays and stories throughout his life and contributed to the St James Gazette and the Yellow Book. He published Pagan Papers in 1893 and the Golden Age in 1895. This latter book told of the games and imaginary heroic adventures he had enjoyed as a child with his brothers and sister. Dream Days was published in 1898, again, looking back on his childhood with great understanding and sensitivity. In that book was a story much loved by children, 'The Reluctant Dragon', a tale about a gentle dragon who was not over-anxious to fight St George.

Grahame retired from the bank through ill-health in 1907 and published the Wind in the Willows in 1908. It began as bedtime stories for his son Alastair and continued in letters when Alastair went to school and was away on holiday. Kenneth Grahame took the stories and added passages of beautiful description. He said it was, "a book of youth, of life, sunshine, running water, woodlands, dusty roads, winter firesides"; a book about all the things he loved. It is a wonderful book with some splendid characters:

- the practical Water Rat. "Believe me,… there is nothing, absolutely nothing, half so much worth doing as simply messing about in boats."
- the humble Mole, who is not impressed by Ratty's song, the Ducks' Ditty. "I don't think very much of that little song, Rat," observed

Mole cautiously. He was no poet himself and didn't care who knew it; and he had a candid nature.

- the pompous Toad. "It's no good Toady; you know well that your songs are all conceit and boasting and vanity; and your speeches are all self-praise and, and, well, and gross exaggeration…." Toad flits from one hobby to another and ends up in prison for stealing a motor car. After the battle of Toad Hall he changes his ways. "Henceforth I will be a very different Toad. My friends, you shall never have occasion to blush for me again. But, O dear, O dear, this is a hard world!"

A.A. Milne, the author of Winnie-the-Pooh, dramatised the Wind in the Willows as Toad of Toad Hall in 1930. Walt Disney turned it into a film called Mr Toad. In the 1980s Cosgrove Hall produced an animated series with David Jason as Mr Toad and in 1995 ITV made a film with Rik Mayall as Toad.

Thought

Imagination is the gift through which we glimpse heaven and see ourselves numbered amongst the saints in glory. Here we can gain insights into our world that simple observation would never grant us. Water Rat, Toad and Mole are imaginary characters that teach us about human nature. Kenneth Grahame's fantasy enhances our reality.

Prayer

God you have blessed us in every age with writers and artists who introduce us to worlds other than our own. Through Kenneth Grahame you have deepened our understanding of nature, and of our own human nature. You have given us amusement and enhanced our lives. Help us to appreciate the gift of imagination with which you have enriched us. And help us to use this gift for the good of all. Through Christ our Lord. Amen.

Open our minds, Lord, to all you want us to understand.
Open our ears, Lord, to all you want us to hear.
Open our eyes, Lord, to all you want us to see.
Open our hearts, Lord, to all whom you want us to love. Amen.

Captain Oates

16 March

Robert Falcon Scott was the leader of British expeditions to the South Pole in 1901-4 and in 1910-12. Scott and Shackleton were in competition against the Norwegian explorers Nansen and Amundsen and Peary the American. The 1910 expedition was an attempt to be first to the South Pole. In spite of bad planning and bad luck at the beginning of 1912, Scott's expedition was within 200 miles of its objective. Scott set out with four others, Dr Wilson, Capt L.E.G. Oates of the Inniskilling Dragoons, Lieut. H.R. Bowers and Petty Officer Edgar Evans. These five were never seen alive again. Scott kept a diary which was later found on his body. They reached the Pole on 18th January, only to find a Norwegian flag already there; Amundsen had beaten them by a month.

The party set out on their tragic return journey. They were seriously delayed by blizzards, one of which lasted for nine whole days. Evans fell and was injured, and eventually died at Beardmore on 17th February. Captain Oates his nickname was Titus – had frostbite in his feet. Scott's diary tells us of his great bravery:

6th March: Oates is wonderfully plucky as his feet must be giving him great pain. He makes no complaint but he grows more silent in his tent.

7th March: A little worse I fear. One of Oates's feet very bad this morning: he is wonderfully brave. We still talk of what we will do together at home.

8th March: Worse and worse in morning; poor Oates's left foot can never last out.

On the 16th and 17th of March Oates declared that he could not go on. At night he grew worse and everyone knew that the end had come. "We can testify to his bravery," wrote Scott. "He has borne intense suffering for weeks without complaining. He did not, would not, give up until the very end. He slept through the night before last hoping not to wake; but he woke in the morning, yesterday. It was blowing a blizzard. He said, 'I am just going outside and may be some time.' He went out into the blizzard and we have not seen him since. It was the act of a brave man and an English gentleman. We all hope to meet the end with similar spirit, and assuredly the end is not far."

The final entry in the diary was for 29th March. Scott, Wilson and Bowers had struggled on another 20 miles and were only 11 miles from a big food depot at One Ton Camp. They had not eaten for eight days and they died of starvation and exposure. Eight months later on 12th November, 1912, a search party found the tent and the frozen bodies. Captain Oates's body was never found. *Captain Oates had walked willingly to his death to give his comrades a better chance of survival. He was indeed, a gallant gentleman.*

Thought

Bravery is unreasonable: attempting what our reason says is foolish, but what a higher reason says is good. Bravery requires strength of spirit, moral resolve and courage, all signs of the presence of God's Holy Spirit. Captain Oates showed all of these traits, quietly sacrificing his own life that his companions might live. He did not save his friends, but his bravery continues to inspire us.

Prayer

Lord, let the example of the brave inspire us to bravery ourselves. May we be strong in spirit, unselfish in our motivation and courageous in our deeds. In serving you, make us joyful, that nothing will be too much for us to undertake. In our friends, you give us companions who will help and support us; we thank you for all those who enrich our lives in so many ways. Thank you for all your gifts, given through Jesus, our companion and our friend. Amen.

Let us imitate the courageous, that we may serve others well.
Let us be strong in times of trial.
Let us be inspired in the decisions we make.
Let us live well, and find joy in being alive.

St Patrick

17 March

Little is known about St Patrick, the apostle of Ireland. Written accounts are late, and there are a great number of legends about him. Where he was born is disputed; anywhere from northern France to the Clyde. His date of birth is about 390.

When he was about fifteen or sixteen Patrick was carried off to Ireland by a band of Irish raiders. He was enslaved and made to look after sheep and pigs, in the area of Antrim. With lots of spare time he began to think about God. "Constantly I used to pray in the daytime. My faith grew and my spirit stirred. I said as many as a hundred prayers a day and as many at night."

Patrick was either freed or he escaped and sailed to Gaul where he trained for the priesthood. Patrick returned to Ireland, as bishop, in about the year 435. He worked mainly in the north, setting up his see at Armagh. He realised that he needed the goodwill of the tribal kings and chieftains. The most powerful leader was the High King of Tara. As Easter approached Patrick decided to spend it at Tara, "which was the chief abode of idolatry and wizardry in Ireland". The king had ordered that all fires should be put out and should be relit from a fire at the king's castle. Anyone who disobeyed should be put to death. Patrick deliberately lit the paschal fire, was seized and brought to the king. He explained that Jesus was the light of the world, and after lengthy argument Christianity was tolerated. The King, Laoghaine, continued to oppose Patrick for nearly 30 years, but eventually was baptised. Patrick and his followers travelled throughout Ireland founding churches and forming communities of monks and nuns.

Patrick died at Saul, on Strongford Lough, in about 461. He was probably buried there.

Patrick wrote a great deal and perhaps his best known words are a hymn called The Deer's Cry:

Christ to protect me today against every poison,
Against burning, against drowning, against death-wound,
So that I may have a multitude of rewards.
Christ with me, Christ before me, Christ behind me,
Christ in me, Christ below me, Christ above me,
Christ at my right, Christ at my left,
Christ in breadth, Christ in length, Christ in height,
Christ in the heart of every one who thinks of me,
Christ in the mouth of every one who speaks to me,
Christ in the eye of every one that sees me,
Christ in the ear of every one that hears me.
I bind myself today to a strong virtue, an invocation of the Trinity.
I believe a Threeness with confession of a Oneness in (the) Creator of
   the Universe.
Salvation is the Lord's, salvation is the Lord's, salvation is Christ's.
May Thy salvation, Lord, be always with us! Amen.

This hymn is now known as Saint Patrick's Breastplate.

Thought

By lighting the Easter fire, Patrick proclaimed the Lordship of the risen Christ. The fire bears witness to the Light which shines in the darkness, the Light which the darkness cannot overcome. Christ is the Light, and in him there is no darkness. When we doubt, or are afraid, when we are lost or in despair, when we are weak or lonely, Christ is our Light, bringing us peace.

Prayer

Lord Christ, when we are alone and afraid, when we are sad and lose hope, when we are lost and confused, let your light shine in us, that we might have the comfort and strength your presence brings. May your light drive all darkness from us, and may we in turn be a light to others, guiding them on their way. We ask this through you, the Light of the World, you who live with the Father and the Holy Spirit, one God for ever and ever. Amen.

Banish our darkness with the light of your presence.
Shine in our world, the Light for all to see.
Help us to live as children of the light
now and always.

Mothering Sunday

The fourth Sunday in Lent is called Mothering Sunday, and is half way through Lent. It is a time for a slight relaxation of Lenten fasting and austerity. Sometimes it is called Laetare Sunday because the opening words of the Latin mass for this Sunday are 'Laetare Jerusalem', 'Rejoice Jerusalem'. This Sunday is also sometimes called 'Refreshment Sunday', either because of the relaxation of fasting or because the gospel for the day, still in the Book of Common Prayer, is the feeding of the five thousand.

The Romans had a festival of Juno, the birth goddess, in March. It was called Matronales Feriae, or Matronalia and married women processed to the temple of Juno and made offerings to the goddess. Small cakes made of extra-fine white flour called simila were offered to the goddess. In the home, prayers were offered for marital happiness. Wives received gifts from their husbands and gave a feast for female slaves. This may be the origin of Mothering Sunday; the Church turned the festival into a time to honour Mother Church, the spiritual mother of all Christians. It became the custom for all Christians in a parish (where there might be several churches or chapels-at-ease), to go to the main parish church on this Sunday.

In the eighteenth and nineteenth centuries servants and apprentices were allowed home on this Sunday, to visit their mothers. They would take home gifts of flowers and cakes. The cake was a Simnel cake, of which there are several varieties. All were made from fine flour, currants, peel, spice, and marzipan. On the top of the cake were often put 11 marzipan eggs, symbolising the apostles without Judas. Sometimes 12 eggs were put on the top, but one had to be coloured black to represent the traitor. The word Simnel probably comes from the Latin word "simila", the fine flour used to bake the cake. There is a story that the first Simnel cake was made by an old couple called Simon and Nell. They quarrelled over how to cook the cake, whether it should be baked or boiled. Eventually they compromised, boiling it first and then baking it afterwards. Again they quarrelled over what to call the cake, and again they compromised, calling it Sim-nell cake, which shortened to Simnel.

In Britain, Mothering Sunday and Mother's Day have become synonymous. Mother's Day was started in America, by Miss Anna Jarvis of Philadelphia, on the first anniversary of the death of her mother, 9th May 1907. The idea of having a special day to remember and honour mothers spread. The Commonwealth of Pennsylvania declared the second Sunday in May to be Mother's Day, and in 1913 the United States Government dedicated that day 'to the memory of the best mother in the world, 'Your mother'. In Britain Mothering Sunday never occurs in May, but it is a great opportunity to thank mothers for all that they do. It is a time to thank God for the joys of family life and to thank him for all the love that we have been given.

Thought

Mothering is about having children and bringing them up; but it is about so much more: giving birth, nurturing, life, development, education and growth. Each person, male or female, can develop the mothering side of their nature, becoming more rounded individuals. We can pray for mothers, that the Lord will bless them and give them all they need; and we can pray for ourselves, that we nurture and help others to grow.

Prayer

Loving God, help all mothers. Be with them in all they have to do; assist them in all they say; love them each and every day. May we grow in gentle strength; may our patience increase; may we persevere, even in adversity; may we help those more needy than ourselves; may we be loving in all our dealings, and be an example for others to follow. We can only ask this knowing of your tender mercy. Amen.

Bless mothers, this day and every day
Bless fathers, in every way
Bless families with unity and peace
Bless all your people
May your blessing never cease

William Booth

10 April

When he was young William Booth knew what it was like to be poor. His father went bankrupt and died early. William was apprenticed to a Nottingham pawnbroker. In 1844 he underwent a conversion experience and became a Methodist minister. In 1849 he moved to London. In 1852 he left the Church with a group of people who later became known as the Methodist New Connection. William became the minister, and married one of the congregation, Catherine Mumford. He broke away from the Anglican Church in 1861 and became an independent revivalist, preaching to the very poor. Catherine preached too, doing much good work in Gateshead, Durham.

William worked with the very poor in London's East End and in 1865 renamed his society the Christian Mission. He and his helpers worked hard to relieve the poor and deprived in Whitechapel. William was convinced that he was fighting a war against poverty and evil, so in 1878 he renamed his Mission as the Salvation Army. He modelled it on military lines; William was the general, his officers were given military ranks, and its members were called soldiers. From the beginning the Salvation Army had bands which led the hymn singing at meetings. The Army worked hard to help the poor and lonely and for a time it was laughed at. The government sometimes found it a nuisance and some of its members were fined or imprisoned for causing disturbances.

In 1890 William published a book called In Darkest England. In it he wrote about the terrible conditions which the poor lived in. The Salvation Army continued its good work and came to be respected by the public. It grew and spread to Europe and to the United States.

Salvation Army members follow the general beliefs of the Protestant churches, but they have no sacraments because they believe that the whole of life is a sacrament. Their services have always included joyful singing, instrumental music, hand-clapping, personal testimony, free prayer and an open invitation to repentance. There is a strong emphasis on helping others; the Salvation Army runs nearly 5,000 social service centres, institutions, maternity homes, children's homes and schools.

Catherine died in 1890 and William himself went blind; but his energy and organising ability remained to the end of his life. When he died in 1912 his work had spread into 59 countries. Today the Salvation Army has branches in 90 countries and has more than 25,000 officers, organised in over 14,000 corps.

William Booth changed many people's lives for the better. When he died he passed his generalship to his son, Bramwell Booth (1856-1\9). Bramwell's sister Evangeline Cory Booth (1865-1950) headed and expanded the Salvation Army in the United States (1904-1934).

Thought

With a vision of justice and compassion, organised in the service of the Lord, the Salvation Army has proclaimed the Reign of God in word and deed. William Booth lived his service of the Lord in a spirit of joyful praise. Happy are those, like him, who help their neighbour in need, give praise to God, and believe the promise made them that eternal life will be theirs.

Prayer

Lord God, help us to be organised in your service, that we may work well to bring your peace to our troubled world, your justice to our divided societies, your healing to our brokenness. Let us work together with all people of good will, that the vision of goodness which we share will be realised. When we work, prompt us to pray, and when we pray, prompt us to work in your service. We ask this through Christ our Lord. Amen.

May we follow Christ our leader with courage.
May we work with Christ our leader for justice.
May we imitate Christ our leader in our zeal for God's kingdom.
May Christ be amongst us and with us, each and every day. Amen.

St George

23 April

St George is a very popular saint! He is the patron saint of England, Portugal, Catalonia, Aragon, Venice and Genoa! Yet almost nothing is known about him. He was born in Cappadocia, now a part of Turkey, and he became a soldier, eventually rising to the rank of Tribune. He became a Christian when the Roman authority was fairly tolerant. Then came persecution under the Emperor Diocletian. Notices were put up warning Christians that they would be tortured if caught, and if they refused to give up their faith then they would be executed. George tore down one of these notices at Nicomedia, near Istanbul, was arrested, tortured, and put to death on the 23rd April, 303.

The dragon came into the story about 600 years later. The word "dragon" comes from the Greek "drakon", which means a large serpent. Dragons appear in many mythologies and are sometimes good and sometimes bad. The Egyptian god Apophis was the great serpent of the world of darkness. It spread darkness over the earth each night and was overcome by the sun god Ra each morning. One tradition makes George's dragon white, with bat-like wings. The early Church regarded dragons as symbols of evil, so the fight between George and the dragon is a fight between good and evil.

The story goes like this: the dragon lived in a swamp and demanded to be fed, two sheep at a time. When the sheep were all gone a human sacrifice had to be offered. The victims were chosen by lot and eventually the king's daughter was chosen. Dressed as a bride she was tied to a tree to wait for the dragon's meal time. Luckily George was passing; he attacked the dragon and wounded it. The princess took the white cord from her waist, tied it round the dragon's neck, and led it into the city. The citizens were so frightened that they promised they would become Christians if George killed the dragon. He did so, and the body was taken away on four ox-carts, to be lost in the swamps forever. About 15,000 men were baptised, not counting women and children.

In the eleventh and twelfth centuries the crusaders brought back stories of how St George had appeared from heaven and had driven back the infidels with celestial darts, first supporting William the Conqueror's son Robert, and later Richard the Lionheart. Richard encouraged his troops to accept George as their patron, and many soldiers put a red cross on their shields. Until that time England's patron had been St Edward the Confessor. In 1222 George became England's patron. Later, Edward III founded the order of the Knights of St George, usually called the Order of the Garter (1349). St George was patron of the Order and St George's Chapel, Windsor was founded in his honour.

St George is the patron saint of soldiers and sailors and the protector of rocky and dangerous coasts, and places liable to flood. His assistance is also invoked for the mentally infirm. It is possible that the rose became the emblem of St George because he fought with the Roman army in Persia – where there were roses in abundance.

Thought

According to legend, St George slew a dragon and delivered people from mortal peril. In this, he is a sign of Jesus Christ, who delivers us from death. Wherever there is oppression and evil, the Christian is called to bear witness to liberty and goodness; and in proclaiming to others the power of Christ, the Christian works for the salvation of the world. Our desire to save others can overcome our fear of defeat; by grace we are victorious.

Prayer

God, let our vigilance against evil be unceasing. Help us grow in goodness, so that we will never rest in the face of oppression. May we see every injustice and hurt to our neighbour as wounding the body of Christ, and may we respond with words and deeds that restore and heal. May we never be afraid of speaking out for the rights and dignity of others. We ask this in the strength of Jesus Christ, in whose death and resurrection we find our hope. Amen.

May the Lord of hosts guard us.
May the God of justice inspire us.
May the Prince of peace unite us. Amen.

St Catherine of Siena

29 April

Catherine was born in Siena, Italy on the feast of the Annunciation, 1347. She had a twin sister who died soon after birth. She was the youngest of 25 children of Giacomo Benincasa, a well-to-do dyer, and his wife, Lapa. When she was six years old she had a vision of Jesus in glory, and that mystical experience sealed her vocation.

When she was twelve her parents urged her to take more care of her appearance. Her parents wished her to marry, but she was determined to enter an order of sisters who were bound by vows but who lived at home. She cut off her golden-brown hair, much to the annoyance of her parents who made her do all the menial work of the house and, because she loved privacy, did not allow her to be alone. She accepted all of her punishments patiently and her father realised that opposition was useless. He gave his permission for her to become a sister.

At first she lived as a recluse in one room, but after three years an inward voice told her to go out into the world. She went out and nursed the sick in hospital. She worked many miracles of healing. During the plague of 1374 she heard that the director of the hospital had caught the disease. She walked in and cheerfully said to him, "Get up, Father Matthew, this is no time to be lying idle in bed." He got up, had a meal, and was cured.

Catherine based her life on love, and she tried to express her beliefs in her Dialogue and in her letters. She dictated everything because she could not write. Her personal holiness was enhanced by her gentle reaction to criticism and ingratitude. She was urged to forget about helping the ungrateful. She replied, "Do you think that our Lord would be pleased with us if we left works of mercy undone because our neighbour is unthankful?" About this time she had a vision of Jesus holding a crown of gold in one hand and a crown of thorns in the other. Jesus asked her to choose one crown, and unhesitatingly she took the crown of thorns.

Catherine spent long hours in prayer and contemplation. In February 1375 she visited Pisa and after receiving communion in the little church of St Christina she meditated whilst looking at the crucifix. Suddenly there seemed to come from it five blood-red rays, which pierced her hands, feet and heart. She found the experience so painful she fainted. The wounds remained with her and were clearly visible after her death.

In the last five years of her life Catherine became involved in the politics of both church and state. She became famous as a peacemaker, and was called on to settle disputes. Four hundred of her letters survive, to Popes, Kings, magistrates and to private people. She attempted to make peace between Florence and the Pope who lived in Avignon, and was one of many who urged Gregory XI to return to Rome. In 1376 the Pope returned to Rome.

After the death of Gregory XI came the Great Schism. Urban VI was elected Pope in Rome and a rival Pope was set up in Avignon. Christendom was divided and Catherine wore herself out trying to obtain the recognition for Urban which was his due. She wrote also to Urban, sometimes to urge fortitude, sometimes to admonish him for his harshness. Far from resenting her reproof, the Pope invited her to Rome, where she worked indefatigably for his cause. Early in 1380 Catherine had a seizure, and then on 21st April she had a stroke which disabled her from the waist downwards. On 29th April she died, aged thirty-three. She was made a saint by Pope Pius II in 1461, and declared a doctor of the Church in 1970.

Thought

To retreat into prayer can be the most radical way to engage with everyday life. To be immersed in prayer is to be in deep conversation with God who is infinitely concerned with all people. And this conversation with God can only lead to the person who prays becoming more involved in service of neighbour. So pray to enter more deeply into service, and serve to be more deeply engaged with God in prayer.

Prayer

Dear God, make us enthusiastic; make us energetic; make us zealous; make us committed; make us faithful; make us imaginative; make us visionary; make us tireless; make us joyful; make us hopeful; make us tolerant; make us lively; make us enthusiastic; make us understanding; make us fearless: all in the service of your Son, Jesus Christ, who came that we might have fullness of life. Amen.

Catherine was determined to serve you: help us to be the same.
Catherine was devoted to those in need: may we follow her example.
Catherine loved you intensely: grant that we might do likewise.
Amen.

Palm Sunday

Today begins the last week of Jesus' life. It is the one week when Christians have a detailed diary of what Jesus did. We call him Jesus Christ, but Christ was not his surname, which would have been bar or ben Joseph, son of Joseph. "Christ" is the Greek word for the Hebrew word "Messiah". Both words mean the anointed one, the one set apart to do something special. Kings and prophets were anointed, also. At the time of Jesus most people were hoping that a political Messiah would come, who would defeat the Romans, occupying Israel, and make the country independent and free. There was an independence movement led by the Zealots; their extreme branch were called the Sicarii or 'long knives', referring to the way they assassinated Romans and collaborators.

Jesus had few possessions, so he borrowed a donkey to ride on as he travelled the last steep bit of road as he approached the Mount of Olives from the east. He had told two disciples to go into an unnamed village and bring back a donkey that had never been ridden. If anyone challenged them they were to say that, "The Master, [the Greek word can mean owner], needs it." The disciples brought the donkey to Jesus and put cloaks over the animal to act as a saddle. So Jesus entered Jerusalem, not as a political Messiah on a war horse, but on a donkey, possibly to fulfil the prophecy of Zechariah 9:9:

> Rejoice, rejoice, people of Zion!
> Shout for joy you people of Jerusalem!
> Look, your King is coming to you!
> He comes triumphant and victorious,
> but humble and riding on a donkey,
> on a colt, the foal of a donkey.

The road Jesus travelled was a busy one, and many people were going to Jerusalem to celebrate the Passover. The crowds joined in the cheering that the disciples no doubt began. They called out "Hosanna!" which means "Save me, I pray!" It was the greeting for the Messiah.

Added to this was the blessing upon pilgrims entering the city: "May God bless the one who comes in the name of the Lord! From the Temple of the Lord we bless you" (Psalm 118:26). The Psalmist goes on to say: "The Lord is God; he has been good to us. With branches in your hands, start the festival and march round the altar" (Psalm 118:27).

Indeed, the crowd cut branches from the palm trees, and waved them and threw them down on the road. It was a carnival atmosphere, but it was not long before the cheers turned to jeers. Jesus was to be rejected in favour of political nationalism which would eventually lead to war with the Romans, and the destruction of the Temple and much of Jerusalem. Today, many Christians are given a palm cross to keep to remind them of the beginning of this Holy Week.

Thought

We cannot always recognise goodness when we encounter it: our fallen nature distorts our vision, Sometimes, we glimpse goodness, but fail to grasp the fullness of the truth that is before us. The people were waiting for the Messiah; they had been waiting for generations. When he came, their welcome was a mixed one; waving palm branches upon his entry to Jerusalem, watching as he was condemned and put to death. Our approach to life can be similarly ambivalent and confused.

Prayer

God of love, help us to recognise goodness and to appreciate it wherever we may find it. Remove what distorts and clouds our vision, that we might see what is true and good and, in doing so, become wise. May we welcome Jesus as our King, preparing his way, greeting him and serving him. In opening our hearts and lives to him, may we become more like him, who lives and reigns with you and the Holy Spirit. Amen.

Jesus, come to us, that we might be saved.
Jesus, rule over us, that we might live in peace.
Jesus, hear our prayers, that we might live for ever. Amen.

Maundy Thursday

"And now I give you a new commandment: love one another. As I have loved you, so you must love one another." (John 13:34) The Latin word 'mandatum' means 'command'; the French equivalent is 'mande', from which comes the English word 'Maundy'. On that Thursday night Jesus commanded the disciples to love one another. He had already shown his love in a great act of humility and service; he had washed the feet of the disciples. (John 13:1-15). In households that had slaves, the youngest, most inexperienced slave sat at the door with a bowl of water. He removed the shoes of the guests and washed their feet as they came into the house. On this occasion the Master washes the feet to show his love, to give an example to follow, and as an act of ritual cleansing. Peter objected and had to have the reason for the exercise explained to him.

Jesus showed his love in a second way, by giving himself in the Holy Eucharist, an act which enshrined his whole love for his Father in heaven and for his friends on earth. The Eucharist is the memorial of Jesus' total self-giving on the Cross, and the principal means by which his saving love is passed on to Christians.

Just as Jesus took a piece of bread and thanked God for it, broke it, and gave it to the disciples, so the priest does today. He uses Jesus' words, "Take it, this is my body." Just as Jesus took a cup of wine, thanked God for it and gave it to the disciples to drink, so the priest does today. Again he uses Jesus' own words, "This is my blood which is poured out for many." Just as the disciples re-enacted the Last Supper to remember Jesus and what he had done for them, so we Christians do the same today.

After the meal Jesus went out of Jerusalem, into the Garden of Gethsemane. (Gethsemane means 'oil-press', and there are olive trees growing there today which were there when Jesus was alive.) There Jesus prayed fervently that the cup of suffering might be taken away from him. It was not removed and Jesus accepted it, "Yet not what I want, but what you want" (Mark 14:36). Then Judas Iscariot arrived with a hired rabble to arrest Jesus. He kissed Jesus, which was the customary greeting for a Rabbi from a disciple. It served to identify

Jesus in the dark, so that the right person could be arrested. The disciples fled.

Jesus was taken away to the High Priest's house. Caiaphas questioned him, with some of the members of the Sanhedrin, the great Jewish Council of 70 members. Outside Peter denied three times that he even knew Jesus. Jesus had been left alone, deserted and denied.

After the Eucharist is over on Maundy Thursday, the Blessed Sacrament is sometimes taken to a side chapel made to look like a garden. The congregation sometimes keep watch before the Blessed Sacrament after the church has been stripped of all decorations. The mood has changed from celebration to sadness, as we look towards Jesus' suffering and death.

Thought

Doing what we are told can be an act of sullen obedience, or a willing response to an invitation. When Jesus told his disciples to love one another, he clearly had their best interests at heart; it would benefit them, and the whole world, if his example of love were to spread. So this command of his is one to which we can respond generously and whole-heartedly. We watch what he does, learn from him, and ask for the grace to do likewise.

Prayer

Loving God, you have given us the example of Jesus to show us how we might live at peace with you and with every person. We cannot always live as we would like to live, and so we look to you for help and strength. Bless our efforts to live well, give us the gift of inner peace, keep us strong in hope and faith, and grant us loving hearts that we might love each other as your Son loves us. We ask this in the name of Jesus, who loved us to the point of death, and loves us still. Amen.

God, we see your love in the face of Jesus your well-beloved Son.
God, we hear your words of love spoken to us in the Scriptures.
God, we know in our heart you love us each and every day.
Guard us, guide us, keep us yours, for ever and ever. Amen.

Good Friday

Good Friday is a very solemn time, a day of mourning, a day of fasting. There may be a long service from noon until 3 p.m. to remember Jesus dying on the cross. The churches are empty and bare; there are no flowers or decorations.

After he had been arrested in the Garden of Gethsemane, Jesus was taken from the High Priest's house and in the morning brought before the Roman governor, Pontius Pilate. Pilate was the only person who could order crucifixion. He questioned Jesus but was not convinced that he was guilty of being a political messiah. In his gospel Luke says that Pilate sent Jesus to King Herod Antipas. Jesus would not speak to Herod and was sent back to Pilate. The gospels say that there was a custom that one man could be released as a goodwill gesture at Passover time. Pilate offered to release either Jesus or a thief and murderer called Barabbas. The crowd called for him to release Barabbas. Matthew says that Pilate washed his hands of the whole business (Matthew 27:24).

Crucifixion was the punishment for slaves and non-Romans. It took a number of forms. Sometimes there was an upright with a crosspiece, sometimes without. Sometimes nails were used to hold the victim as well as ropes. The punishment was degrading; the victim was usually naked and might survive for some days. After death the body was usually left to rot as a sign to warn others not to ignore the might of the Roman Empire.

Before crucifixion the victim was scourged. A scourge is a whip with several thongs, each thong having pieces of metal or bone along its length, which cut into the skin. Jesus was soundly scourged by the soldiers, who mocked him as 'King of the Jews', and then took him to the place of execution. Read the gospel passage now. In his account of the death of Jesus, St John says that the Jewish authorities were keen that the bodies should not be displayed on the Sabbath day. To speed up the death of the victims the soldiers broke the legs of the thieves. This was to prevent them easing the strain on their chest and arms. When their strength gave way they suffocated quickly. Jesus was already dead but, to make sure, one of the soldiers stabbed him through the heart with his spear.

Joseph of Arimathea, a secret disciple of Jesus, was given permission by Pilate to bury Jesus' body. Joseph had the corpse wrapped in linen with about 30 kilogrammes of myrrh and aloes, (John 19:39-40), and put in the tomb he had prepared for his own burial. John's gospel says that Joseph was helped by Nicodemus. The women who had followed Jesus and witnessed his death went with Joseph and Nicodemus and saw where the body had been placed.

That is the story of Good Friday. But why Good Friday? Perhaps it means God's Friday or possibly holy Friday. For Christians it is the day that Jesus died to save the world from sin, "For God loved the world so much that he gave his only son, so that everyone who believes in him may not die but have eternal life" (John 3:16).

Thought

Good Friday is a bleak day, a celebration of a famous death. Yet it is called good. How can something fateful, hopeless and bleak, also be something good? In itself, it cannot be good; but in context, it is good indeed. Good Friday is not simply a celebration of failure and death, but a scene-setting for what comes after: the blazing glory of the resurrection of Jesus from the dead. But for now, let us stay with the bleakness, with the death. Let us mourn for the frustration of all our hopes. Knowing that this is not the end of the story.

Prayer

Eternal God, you are at the dawn of time, and at the end of time, and at every moment of time; your Son Jesus united himself with our humanity, that he might share our frustration and pain, and that we might share his healing and hope. What he shares of our life, may he redeem; what we share of his life may we treasure. We ask this through the same Jesus Christ our Lord, who remains faithful to you and to us, for ever and ever. Amen.

When despair, darkness and death comes close,
may hope, light and life save us.
When all seems lost and we have nowhere to go,
may Jesus be our consolation.
When so much seems bad and evil wins the day,
show us goodness and the triumph of your love. Amen.

Holy Saturday

On Holy Saturday night the Church keeps the Easter vigil. We wait at the Lord's tomb, meditating upon his suffering and death but confident in the knowledge that God's love is stronger than death.

The Service begins in darkness and is divided into four parts:
The Service of Light.
The Liturgy of the Word.
The Celebration of Baptism.
The Liturgy of the Eucharist.

The Service of Light:

All gather outside the church where a new fire is lit and blessed. From this fire the Easter candle is lit. The candle is also known as the paschal candle, from the Latin translation of the Hebrew word for Passover. Easter and Passover are linked. The people process into the darkened church behind the deacon who carries the paschal candle. The light then spreads out as the people light their own candles from the paschal candle. Three times the deacon stops and sings the proclamation, "The light of Christ." The people reply, "Thanks be to God." When he reaches the sanctuary the deacon places the candle on its stand and sings the Easter Proclamation, a song of thanks and joy for all the wonders God has worked, especially his raising Jesus from the dead.

The Liturgy of the Word:

There can be up to seven Old Testament lessons, each dealing with some aspect of God's great creative and redemptive activity. After each reading there is a pause for reflection and prayer. When the last reading is finished the priest intones the Gloria, all the lights are put on, the bells are rung and the organ plays for the first time since Holy Thursday. All join in the Church's great hymn of rejoicing, Glory to God in the highest! The service follows the usual format of Collect,

Scripture Readings, etc to the sermon.

The Celebration of Baptism:

In the early Church people who wanted to become Christians went through a period of instruction and were called Catechumens. At church services the Catechumens stayed for the readings and sermon but left before the eucharistic service began. The Easter vigil was the usual time for baptisms. On this solemn night the catechumens heard the word of God and then received the new life of Christ through the water of baptism and the power of the Holy Spirit. Their joy was made complete as they took part for the first time in the Easter mass. Some churches have re-introduced the catechumenate and the candidates are baptised at the Easter vigil. If there is no one to be baptised, after blessing the baptismal water in the font, the priest invites all the people present to renew their own baptismal vows.

The Liturgy of the Eucharist:

When the Eucharist was celebrated on Holy Thursday it had an air of sadness about it. It was a re-enactment of Jesus' last meal with his disciples before he was arrested and killed. He was going away. Now the celebration is filled with joy, for the Lord has returned, as he said he would. He is risen indeed!

Thought

Holy Saturday is a day of waiting. After the solemn celebration of the death of Jesus on Good Friday, we wait at the tomb, watching and praying. We know the day will end in glory, but still we watch and wait. In the tomb are our hopes and our dreams seemed to die with Jesus, but with him, they will arise. Waiting for the glory of the Lord is an apt description of the Christian life, and Holy Saturday is a sacrament, a sign of waiting. Joyful hope characterises the waiting of those who believe.

Prayer

Lord, be with us as we keep vigil at the tomb of Jesus your Son. Let us wait in hope for his resurrection from the dead, knowing that in his life is our life. When we are discouraged or in despair, when we are sad and cannot see a way forward, let the risen life of Jesus Christ fill us with new life and hope. As we watch and wait, so let our efforts be rewarded, and let our hearts sing of the presence of our Lord, risen from the tomb.

Jesus, you who became like us, that you might save us, have mercy on us.
Jesus, you who died for us, and in dying showed us your great love,
have mercy on us.
Jesus, you who rested in death for three days, and then rose again,
have mercy on us.
Rising Lord, raise us up, and in your mercy show us your glory.
Amen.

Easter

For Christians Easter is the time when we celebrate that Jesus has risen from the dead; the tomb is empty.

Early on the Sunday, at first light, the women went to the tomb to wash the body and to finish embalming it. Mark says that an angel told the women that Jesus had been raised from the dead. They ran away distressed and terrified and told no one. John's gospel says that Mary Magdalene found the tomb empty and ran and told Peter and John. They ran to the tomb, and John, who was fitter, got there first. He saw the linen cloth that had been wrapped round Jesus' body and the separate cloth that had been round the head. Then Peter arrived and rushed into the tomb. They went back to the house where they were staying.

Mary Magdalene stood crying outside the tomb. She believed that someone had taken the body away. She saw someone whom she believed to be the gardener. Only when he spoke to her did she recognise him as Jesus. She went and told the disciples what she had seen and what Jesus had said.

Jesus appeared to Peter, to two of the disciples on the road to the village of Emmaus, and to all the disciples together, except Thomas. A week later Jesus appeared to the disciples, including Thomas. More appearances happened near the Sea of Galilee. The Lord was risen, he was risen indeed! What about those who say Jesus did not rise from the dead, that the disciples stole the body? It seems very odd that they were prepared to preach and to die themselves for the belief that Jesus was risen if they knew he was dead and had hidden his body.

No one, not even the Jewish authorities produced a body to counter the claim that Jesus was risen. If someone had stolen the body, why were the grave clothes left behind? Jews regarded the touching of a dead person as making them unclean, so it is hardly likely that someone undressed the body to take it away.

There are a number of interesting customs associated with Easter. First the name itself. Some think it comes from the name of the Anglo-Saxon goddess of the dawn, Eastre. Her festival was in the spring and the hare was sacred to her, which may well explain the idea of Easter bunnies.

Why Easter eggs? The egg is a symbol of new life. Eggs had been forbidden during Lent so at Easter people gave eggs as presents to their friends. In Germany homes are sometimes decorated with 'egg trees' at Easter. Branches are put into vases and decorated shells are hung on them. Some places hold egg rolling contests, when hard boiled eggs are rolled down a hill, the prize going to the one whose egg rolls the farthest. Egg rolling is a custom older than Christianity but for Christians it symbolises the rolling away of the stone that covered the entrance to Jesus' tomb.

Thought

We look to the East for the rising of the sun, and in the rising of the sun we are reminded of the resurrection of Jesus Christ from the dead. No morning sunrise can match the brilliance of that morning when he rose. All goodness that had seemed lost for ever, was rescued by him. His rising was not just the saving of one person from the dead, but the opening of the gates of life to all; once Jesus had conquered death, then no-one need die again. They would still die to this life on earth, but now they would be born to everlasting life. Alleluia is a one-word prayer expressing all our thanks and praise for the resurrection of Jesus from the dead.

Prayer

Alleluia! Jesus is alive! Alleluia, he who died, is risen from the dead! Alleluia, he who gave his life for us, now lives for us! Heavenly Father, help us truly to rejoice in the resurrection of Jesus your Son. May Easter joy fill our hearts, and the hearts of all people. May Jesus' Easter greeting, 'Peace be with you', be heard in all places, and take root wherever lives are broken by violence. May those who live in darkness cry 'Alleluia', and may the darkness flee before the light of your Son, who is Lord for ever and ever. Amen.

God, in the resurrection of Jesus from the dead may we be filled with hope.
God, in the resurrection of Jesus from the dead may we be renewed in spirit.
God, in the resurrection of Jesus from the dead may we live for ever.
Through Jesus, who died and is risen, and lives for ever. Amen.

Florence Nightingale

12 May

Hospitals in the nineteenth century were usually filthy, fever-ridden and staffed by untrained nurses. Florence Nightingale was brought up in a well-to-do family in a privileged and sheltered society. When, at the age of seventeen, she told her parents she felt God was calling her to become a nurse they were horrified and refused her. When she later turned down a marriage proposal because she wanted to be a nurse her parents accepted that she was determined on her career.

In 1853, after training, Florence became Lady Superintendent of the Institute for Sick Gentlewomen in London. Her work was so successful that Sidney Herbert, the Secretary of State for War and a personal friend, wrote to ask her to go to the Crimea, where Britain and France were fighting Russia. She had already written to Sidney Herbert offering to go; their letters crossed in the post.

Florence set sail in 1854 with 38 nurses for the British hospital at Scutari, near Constantinople. She found terrible conditions, no medicines, no beds, no bedding, no spare clothing, no soap. The sick and wounded lay crammed next to one another on the floor. There was no hot water and no proper drainage. Doctors were also frustrated by the military red tape that made supplies difficult to get.

Florence was at first treated with suspicion. She had brought medical supplies of her own and was supported by money from The Times newspaper. She supervised the repair and refitting of one wing of the hospital, just in time to receive 800 new patients. Florence often worked 20 hours a day and at night made her rounds carrying a lantern. She often tended the critically-ill herself. The soldiers worshipped her, calling her The Lady with the Lamp and they kissed her shadow as she passed. In January 1855 there were 12,000 patients in Scutari and 42 per cent of them died. Conditions so improved that by June the death rate was reduced to 2 per cent. Florence travelled through the Crimea fitting out and organising other hospitals. The strain upon her was tremendous and she became very ill. She recovered and took up the work again, providing recreation rooms, books and lectures for convalescing officers, and later for ordinary soldiers as well. When the war was over in 1856 Florence waited until all the sick had left hospital before returning home herself.

Although ill and exhausted, Florence started to work to improve conditions in the army at home. The Army Medical School was founded and by 1861 the death rate among the troops had halved.

The public collected £50,000 to help her work and in 1860 Florence founded the Nightingale Training School for Nurses, attached to St Thomas's Hospital in London. Nurses and midwives were trained there to new and higher standards of skill and discipline. Nursing became an honourable profession.

By 1901 Florence was blind but she carried on with her work. In 1907 King Edward VII awarded her the Order of Merit, the first woman to receive it. Her only comment was, "Too kind, too kind." Florence Nightingale died in 1910.

Thought

The healing mission of Jesus continues today in men and women who work with the sick. Wherever people work for the health of others, the healing Spirit of Jesus is present. In Florence Nightingale, Jesus walked amongst the injured and sick, giving comfort, healing and hope. In each and every person who cares for others, Jesus is present. Slowly, certainly, through him the world is being saved. As Jesus himself pointed out, healing is a sign that the Reign of God is already in our midst.

Prayer

Holy Spirit of God, you bring the healing of Jesus to your people through those who care for the sick. Give them new strength, dedication, energy and hope in their healing work, that sickness may be banished and all may have fullness of life. Help each of us to care for others in need, especially those who are sick. Let us be a healing presence to all whom we meet. Give us new faith in your healing, strengthening power. Amen.

Lord Jesus, you give new hope to all who suffer in body, mind or spirit.
Healer of all ills, you are with those who are sick.
Our companion and our friend, you inspire us to continue your healing work.
May we be worthy of our calling to love you and serve you. Amen.

Edward Jenner

14 May

Edward Jenner was the son of a Gloucestershire vicar. He was born in the town of Berkeley on the 17th May 1749. Both his parents died when he was five years old. He left grammar school at the age of thirteen and served an apprenticeship with a doctor near Bristol. At the age of twenty-one he studied medicine at St George's Hospital, London, where he finished his training. He was the pupil of a famous surgeon, John Hunter, and they became lifelong friends. Hunter stimulated Jenner's lively and enquiring mind. At the age of twenty-four Jenner chose to leave London to become a country doctor in his native town.

In the eighteenth century smallpox was a major killer, claiming tens of thousands of lives. In London alone 2000 people died of smallpox every year. Jenner heard a milkmaid claim that she would not get smallpox because she had already had cowpox; the sores on cows' teats sometimes spread to the hands of milkmaids. Jenner studied this proposition carefully for about 20 years. No one knew about germs in those days, but by careful observation Jenner realised that cowpox gave protection against smallpox at a certain stage in its development. To test his hypothesis he performed the first vaccination on the 14th May 1796. The word vaccination comes from the Latin word 'vacca' which means 'a cow'. He inserted the contents of a blistering pustule into two scratches made on the arm of a healthy eight-year-old boy called James Phipps. The boy got cowpox. A few months later Jenner inoculated the boy with smallpox, but he did not become ill. In 1798 Jenner published his findings; they aroused fierce opposition from the medical profession. The public were more enthusiastic and Jenner became famous and rich. Parliament rewarded him with sums totalling £30,000, a huge sum in those days. Emperors sent him presents, and even Napoleon released some prisoners of war because Jenner had requested it.

Jenner loved music and poetry, and wrote some poems about birds.

He discovered, by careful observation, what cuckoos do to remove nestlings and eggs from nests, and he was possibly the first person to realise the importance of the earthworm in the maintenance of healthy, arable soil.

Vaccination against smallpox was compulsory in England until 1948. It was effectively eradicated as a worldwide disease by 1979.

Jenner continued living in Berkeley, carrying on his practice until he died on 26th January 1823, aged seventy-three.

Thought

The enquiring mind is a seed-bed for scientific advance and progress, though not all scientific research contributes to the wellbeing of humankind. The life of Edward Jenner is a wonderful example of an enquiring mind making very important discoveries, benefiting countless millions of people ever since. In the work of people like him, we see God's restless Spirit, inspiring and encouraging, that people might know health and life. Sickness and death were never meant to be, and their eradication by Christ and those who work with him are a sign of the coming Reign of God.

Prayer

Loving God, in the life of Edward Jenner and countless women and men, you show us skills and energy in the service of your people. Let us imitate those who do good, putting our own skills and energy at your disposal. Help us make a difference to our world, bringing goodness and love. Inspire those who work for health and life, that they might bring comfort and hope. We ask this through Jesus your Son, our healer and our friend.

God of life, give us life that we might truly live.
God of goodness, inspire us that we may help others to live.
God of mercy, help us when we are weak, that we might persist in doing good.
God of all, we give you thanks and praise. Amen.

Pierre and Marie Curie

15 May

Pierre Curie was born and brought up in Paris. He was a physicist who was especially interested in magnetism and electricity. His wife Marie Sklodowska, the daughter of a Polish professor of physics and mathematics, was a chemist, interested in minerals and metals. At the age of twenty-four she had saved enough money as a teacher to move to Paris to study science at the Sorbonne, the University of Paris. She worked very hard, in the greatest poverty. She sometimes fainted with hunger during her classes. She met Pierre, and fell in love, and they married in1895.

Late in 1895 Röntgen discovered X-rays, Becquerel discovered that uranium was radioactive in 1896. The Curies were friends of Becquerel and decided to work together on this new, exciting subject. Marie invented a special form of electroscope for comparing the radiation given off by different substances. They knew that the element uranium gave off energy continuously and that the energy could electrify the air. They found out that pitchblende, the ore from which uranium is obtained, was many times more radioactive than uranium itself. From tons of pitchblende they managed to obtain a small teaspoonful of something that was thousands of times more radioactive than uranium. After careful analysis the Curies realised that they had discovered two new elements which resembled bismuth and barium chemically, but which could not be, because they were not known to be radioactive. From the bismuth Marie separated a radioactive element which she called polonium, in honour of her native Poland, and from the barium a radioactive element which she called radium.

All this was done when the Curies were poor and hardly known. Their laboratory was an old store-room in the University, basically a shed that did not keep out wind or rain. They lived in poor quarters with their one-year-old daughter, and often did not have enough to eat because they spent their money on apparatus.

In 1900 Pierre became professor of physics at the Sorbonne. In 1903 the Curies and Antoine Becquerel shared the Nobel Prize for physics.

Unfortunately in 1906 Pierre was killed in a street accident in Paris. Marie succeeded him as professor at the Sorbonne. She continued in her researches and in 1911 was awarded the Nobel Prize for chemistry, the first scientist to receive two Nobel Prizes. During the First World War she helped to establish radiological work in hospitals and later became head of the research department of the Radium Institute established by the Sorbonne.

Nothing was known in those days of the dangers of over-exposure to radioactivity. Marie suffered painful burns and her life was shortened by a form of blood disease caused by radioactivity. She died in 1934. The word "curie" is used as a unity of measurement for radioactivity in memory of Pierre and Marie. Their daughter Irene Joliot-Curie also won a Nobel Prize for chemistry.

Thought

The Curies were dedicated to discovering more about the invisible forces of radiation, and putting those forces to work for the good of humankind. Not without suffering themselves, they gave their best efforts to the wellbeing of others. Jesus says that there is no greater love, than if someone lays down their life for their friends; not all ways of doing this are dramatic or obvious. Ordinary men and women daily lay down their lives for others, often receiving little recognition. Pierre and Marie Curie stand as representatives of so many others, many of whose names we will never know.

Prayer

Jesus Christ, you willingly gave your life for us, to save us and to show your love for us. From you we learn the transforming power of love. In the dedicated lives of countless people, we glimpse your love and, glimpsing it, we give thanks for it and desire to imitate it. Help us to live not for ourselves, but for others; in losing ourselves, help us truly to find ourselves. May we ask, each and every day, not 'What can I gain today', but rather, 'What can I give today?' Amen.

God, in your goodness, make us good.
God, in your gentleness, make us gentle.
God, in your great mercy, let us be like you. Amen,

Ascension Day

5 – 4 – 3 – 2 – 1 – Blast off! That is how many people think of
Ascension Day. Jesus disappears into a cloud, perhaps his feet sticking
out of the bottom of it. We all know that God is a spirit, he is not
sitting on a throne out there in space. All Luke was trying to say was
that Jesus had left the earthly scene and had entered the heavenly
domain in power and glory. Space and time are irrelevant to heaven,
neither exist there.

We have here an ending and a beginning. It was the end of Jesus'
earthly mission; our salvation is complete. The way to God, blocked by
sin, is now open; death has been defeated. It is also an end to the post-
resurrection appearances to the disciples. It is the beginning of Jesus'
heavenly ministry; working through the Holy Spirit he is able to
empower the disciples to spread the gospel, the good news.

In his story Luke writes about a cloud, on the Mount of Olives, into
which Jesus disappears. He was using symbolic language. The cloud was
the Shekinah, the cloud that showed the presence of God. It is found at
the Exodus, for example, as well as at Jesus' baptism and his
transfiguration.

When we are baptised we are made part of Christ's body, the
Church. The head of that body is Jesus and he is in heaven. That was
why the disciples were filled with joy and why we should be happy,
too. We are sure to enter heaven some day, as long as we remain
attached to Jesus. For our part we must pray for God's Holy Spirit to
fill our lives, and let it happen.

A legend says that when Jesus returned to heaven the angel Gabriel
asked him what plans he had made to continue his work. "I have left
eleven men behind," Jesus said. "But what if they should fail?" asked
Gabriel. Jesus answered, "I have no other plans. I rely on them."

Thought

Jesus ascended to heaven and could no longer be seen by his disciples. His going was not a true departure, but rather the transition to a new way of being with them; he would send them his Spirit, and be with them throughout their lives, in everything they said and did, each and every moment of each and every day. Jesus leaves the world to enter into glory; once again, in his life we see the promise of our own.

Prayer

Lord God, Jesus rose from the dead and ascended into heaven, showing us what our own destiny would be. Thank you for the promise of glory we have received in your Son. Help us to live with him, to imitate him, to live in the power of his Spirit, and so to ascend with him into the glory that is yours, with Jesus Christ and the same Holy Spirit, one God for ever and ever. Amen.

Lord Jesus, as you are taken from our sight, stay close to us.
Lord Jesus, as you are taken into glory, increase our faith in the Kingdom of your love.
Lord Jesus, as you dwell in us through your Spirit, let us take your presence to others.
Amen.

John and Charles Wesley

24 May

John Wesley was born in Epworth rectory, Lincolnshire, in 1703; his brother Charles in 1707. They were the sons and grandsons of clergymen and followed in their footsteps. John was ordained priest in 1728, Charles in 1735.

John was curate to his father and then went to Oxford as a tutor in Lincoln College. He became the leader of the 'Holy Club' to which Charles also belonged; a group of young men who tried to lead methodical lives; praying and reading the Bible regularly; receiving the sacraments, giving money to the poor and visiting prisoners in Oxford gaol. They were nicknamed 'Methodists'.

In 1735 both John and Charles went to the American colony of Georgia as missionaries. Charles returned to England in 1736; John stayed until 1738. His preaching against drink and slavery did not endear him to the colonists.

On 24th May 1738 John attended a gospel meeting in Aldersgate Street, London. As he listened to the preface to the Epistle to the Romans written by Martin Luther he experienced a religious conversion. He wrote in his journal, "I felt my heart strangely warmed. I felt I did trust in Christ, Christ alone, for salvation; and an assurance was given me that he had taken away my sins, even mine."

John wanted to share the gospel, the good news, with others. He declared, "the world is my parish" and set out on horseback to make the gospel known. For the rest of his life, more than 50 years, he preached his faith all over Great Britain and Ireland. He travelled over 250,000 miles and preached over 50,000 sermons. He once said, "I have so much to do that I must spend several hours in prayer before I am able to do it."

He did not wish to break with the Church of England but many clergy disliked his revivalist approach. He preached in churches when he was allowed to, otherwise he preached anywhere and everywhere.

Sometimes he was mobbed, stoned, spat upon and punched, but he never gave up. Wherever he went he left behind a small band of believers, organised and disciplined, with lay preachers to help evangelise. The Methodists were told to attend Holy Communion in their local churches but they were not always welcome there. John realised that something had to be done to enable Methodist leaders to administer the sacraments. He himself ordained a number of ministers, some of whom went to America. The Church of England would not recognise these orders as valid, and Wesley saw his group become a separate church.

Charles helped his brother and, working from London and Bristol, undertook journeys to preach the gospel. Despite failing health in later life he kept preaching as much as his illness would allow. Charles remained within the Church of England and disapproved of John's ordaining ministers. Charles is probably best remembered for his hymns. He wrote some 6,000 hymns, of which about 500 are still used, including, Jesu, lover of my soul; O, for a thousand tongues to sing; Love divine, all loves excelling; Hark! the herald angels sing; O thou who comest from above.

Charles' son Samuel, 1766-1837, was also a musician, and Samuel's son, Samuel Sebastian Wesley, 1810-1876, was a great organist and composer of church music.

Thought

It is difficult for originality and spontaneity to flourish in institutions, so there is a special role for men and women who can bring these qualities to their place of work or of worship. John and Charles Wesley were prophets, bringing to the Church of their day gifts the Church needed so much. Evident closeness to Christ fuelled the respective ministries of the Wesley brothers: from him they received energy, perseverance, dedication and such a vision of God's love that they could only but preach and sing of what God had revealed to their heart.

Prayer

God, you gave your Holy Spirit to John and Charles Wesley that they might strengthen the faith of those who believed; that they might bring unbelievers to faith; and that your Reign might come on earth. Let that same Spirit speak to our heart that we too may be tireless in singing of your goodness, and telling of your love. We ask this through Christ our Lord. Amen.

Lord, give us a new voice that we might for ever sing your praise.
Give us strong hands that we might do your work on earth.
Give us hearts full of love that we might recognise you in those who are in need.
Amen.

Whit Sunday

Today is the Church's birthday! So today all Christians should have a party. Balloons, bubbles, music! We need them all. But what do all those things need? The answer is, of course, air. If you read the story in Acts of the coming of the Holy Spirit onto and into the disciples then you will see that Luke uses the imagery of wind and fire. He was trying to explain a religious event, using imagery that his readers would understand. The wind was more than air, it was the way Luke described God's Spirit. The disciples came spiritually alive, just as Adam came alive when God breathed life into him in Genesis.

For the Jews, fire made things clean – so the disciples were made clean – (just like Isaiah in Isaiah 6:6-7). But fire also represented the presence of God; the burning bush and the pillar of fire are two Old Testament examples. Luke was saying that God was present in that upper room and had a profound effect on the disciples. They were changed from frightened men into men who went out and boldly preached the gospel, the good news about Jesus. They were changed just as breath changes soap suds into bubbles or a piece of rubber into a balloon, or a piece of wood or plastic into a musical instrument.

If the sun did not shine then our world would cease to exist. There would be no more life, or light, or warmth. Even if the sun is behind the clouds we know that it is there giving warmth and light to the earth. It is a vast ball of fire and it is no real wonder that ancient peoples worshipped it. They were wrong to see it as a god, and we know that God is greater and more powerful than the sun, and the universe too. Fire can give light; it can show the way; it can warm; it can weld; that is why Luke describes the Holy Spirit as fire: God's Spirit can direct us and show us the way; it can make us feel warm, wanted and loved by God; and it can weld or unite us into one great group, the Church, here on earth.

Anyone who has been in a storm knows how powerful the wind can be. It enters anywhere that is open to it. Just so the Holy Spirit. It is unseen but the power is everywhere and is irresistible. All the love and goodness and wisdom and courage in the people is really the Holy Spirit at work in them. God's Spirit will live and work in anyone who is open, and prepared to let the Spirit into their lives. God uses us, ordinary people, to spread love and goodness, and to make this world a better place. This is beautifully summed up by a prayer of St Teresa of Avila:

> *Christ has no body now*
> *on earth but yours.*
> *No hands but yours.*
> *No feet but yours;*
> *Yours are the eyes*
> *   through which is to look out*
> *Christ's compassion to the World;*
> *Yours are the feet*
> *   with which he is*
> *to go about doing good;*
> *Yours are the hands*
> *   with which he is*
> *to bless us now. Amen.*

Just as the Holy Spirit turned the disciples (learners) into apostles (those who are sent out), so that same Holy Spirit can use us to do God's will, if we let it happen!

Thought

The Holy Spirit turns people inside out, changes priorities, dreams and lives. Fearful, inactive disciples found themselves wholly changed: they became powerful, articulate proclaimers of the Gospel of Christ. And so the Gospel isn't just the message: but the people who proclaim it are part of what they proclaim: human beings transformed by the power of God. No longer inhibited by fear, but enthused by the Spirit of the Risen Christ, they are transformed, and in turn they transform others too.

Prayer

Holy Spirit of Jesus, present at the creation of the world, present at the baptism of Christ, sent on the disciples at Pentecost, giving life and bringing peace; fill us now, inspire us, strengthen us, give us the gifts you have promised. Make us part of the Good News of Jesus Christ, so that we are what we proclaim: the love of God made visible, for the salvation of the world. We ask this through Jesus our Lord. Amen.

God, send the Spirit of Jesus upon us that we might know your love.
Jesus, let your Spirit dwell within us that we will know the Truth.
Spirit, make your home in our heart that we might be transformed from within.
One God, bless us and keep us. Amen.

John XXIII

3 June

Angelo Roncalli was born on 25th November 1881, in the tiny village of Sotto il Monte, seven miles from Bergamo, Italy. He was the third child, and eldest son, of a tenant farmer. He had twelve brothers and sisters. The family was poor but had enough to eat and were healthy and happy.

At the age of eleven Angelo began to train for the priesthood. He was ordained priest in Rome on 10th August 1904. During the First World War he served as a hospital orderly and later as a military chaplain. He continued his studies and eventually received a doctorate in canon law. He became the secretary of the Bishop of Bergamo and taught as a professor of theology in the diocesan seminary. After the Bishop's death he was called to join the Vatican's diplomatic service. From 1933-1944 he served as the apostolic visitor to Bulgaria, and apostolic delegate to Greece and Turkey. In 1944 he was made Papal Nuncio to France where his tact, charm and good humour were needed and shown. In 1953 he was appointed cardinal and became the Patriarch of Venice.

When he was almost seventy-seven years old Cardinal Roncalli was elected Pope. It was the 12th ballot and it was obvious that he was a compromise candidate. He would be a 'stop-gap' Pope who would cause no trouble, or so the 51 cardinals thought. During John's reign of 4 years and 7 months there were many changes in the Vatican – both small and large. His warm personality and love of company meant that he refused to eat alone. He disliked pomp and ceremony. He talked to the gardeners in the papal gardens, before this they had to hide or get down on their knees. He ordered that the nobles who carried the papal chair should get more money because of the increased papal weight. He was asked, "How many people work in the Vatican City, Holy Father?" With a twinkle in his eye he answered, "About half". Unlike the popes before him he travelled around Rome, sometimes wearing a black cassock, in the evening. This made a whisky called Johnny Walker popular in Italy! He visited hospitals and prisons. To the prisoners he said, "Since you could not come to me, I came to you."

To the consternation of the conservative cardinals Pope John called the Second Vatican Council into being. There came about sweeping changes in the Church, to bring it up to date. Rules and regulations were relaxed, and the Mass could be said in the native language rather than Latin. There was to be more congregational participation. "I'm the Pope who keeps stepping on the accelerator," John said.

Pope John invited many non-Catholic Christian church leaders to Rome. Christian unity was dear to his heart. He also worked hard to foster international co-operation, especially between communist countries and the West. His warm personality, his unselfishness and his genuine concern for others made 'the roly-poly Pope' one of the best-loved men on earth.

Stories abound about Angelo Roncalli. When he was Archbishop he was invited to a formal dinner where the chief Rabbi of Paris was present. When the time came to go into the meal there was a problem of precedence. The Archbishop immediately assessed the situation and gently pushed the Rabbi forward, with the words, "Old Testament before the New." As Pope John XXIII he met a carpenter who was nearly as plump as himself. "Which Party do you belong to?" the Pope asked. "None, Holy Father," was the reply. "I'm sure you belong to the PMF" said the Pope, laughing. "The Party of Fat Men. You and I are automatic members!"

Pope John died on 3rd June 1963, mourned by millions of people the world over.

Thought

God calls unlikely people to achieve great things. At the beginning of his life, no-one could have imagined the huge changes which would result from the ministry of this one man, John XXIII, yet God used him, and his memory is revered by many Christians. The life of this John teaches us something important about our service of the Lord: God calls, God grants grace, God encourages; and what we begin, God completes. In each of us, and through each of us, God can work miracles of building, healing, caring, renewing and hope.

Prayer

God our loving Father, each of us has a unique purpose in your creation and in your plan of salvation. Help us to discern the part you would have us play; give us the strength we need to serve you; let us encourage each other and work together, that your will be done; bring to conclusion the good works we start in your name. In all things, loving Father, let us give praise to you, to the Holy Spirit, and to Jesus our Saviour. Amen.

God, giver of all good gifts, grant us fullness of life.
God, Spirit of renewal in every age, make all things new.
God, our comfort and our hope, grant us peace.
Amen

Helen Keller

27 June

On 27th June 1880 Helen Keller was born in Tuscumbia, Alabama. She was a beautiful baby, but when she was nineteen months old a serious illness destroyed her sight and hearing. Because she could not hear she could not learn to speak. Her world had become dark and lonely and Helen reacted with violent temper tantrums. In her book The Story of My Life, Helen described herself as wild and unruly. Most people would have given up; most people who met Helen not only thought that she was uncontrollable but that she was stupid.

Her father did not give up, and eventually found someone to help his daughter. On 2nd March 1887, just before Helen was seven, Anne Sullivan arrived to teach her. Anne herself had been nearly blind in childhood but two operations had partially restored her sight.

Anne started to teach Helen by spelling words onto her hand. She gave Helen a doll and spelt out d.o.l.l. on her hand. At first it did not work, but then on 5th April the breakthrough came. "It happened at the well-house, where I was holding a mug under the spout. Annie pumped water into it, and when the water gushed out into my hand she kept spelling w-a-t-e-r into my other hand with her fingers. Suddenly I understood. Caught up in the first joy I had known since my illness, I reached out eagerly to Annie's ever-ready hand, begging for new words to identify whatever objects I touched. Spark after spark of meaning flew from hand to hand and, miraculously, affection was born. From the well-house there walked two enraptured beings calling each other Helen and Teacher. With the help of special schools in New York and Boston, Helen learned to read and write in Braille. Then she learned to speak; by putting her middle finger on the speaker's nose, her forefinger on the lips and her thumb on the speaker's larynx, she then tried to copy the word. At sixteen Helen could communicate well enough to go to private school and then on to College. She graduated with honours from Radcliffe, at Cambridge, Massachusetts in 1904.

Anne was with her all the time, spelling out lectures into Helen's hand and overusing her own poor eyesight to spell out books that were not in Braille. Helen was very intelligent. She mastered five languages, and wrote her first book, The Story of My Life, in 1903.

Helen devoted her life to the blind and deaf-blind. She became active on the staff of the American Foundation for the Blind and the American Foundation for Overseas Blind. She lectured with the help of an interpreter because her voice was not generally intelligible. She wrote many books and articles. In her later years she spent much time helping the blind in developing countries and travelled world-wide. She worked with soldiers who had been blinded in the Second World War, too. To all those she met she gave new courage. In 1964 Helen was awarded the Presidential Medal of Freedom, the highest American civilian award. She died on 1st June 1968.

Thought

Virtue only exists in the virtuous, not in any abstract sense at all; we know what goodness is because we see people who are good. In Helen Keller, we see courage and perseverance. Those around us learn from us, picking up our good attributes and our bad, so our personal struggle for goodness is a shared struggle: we are not simply trying to save our own soul, but working for the salvation of the world. The heroic example of others shows us what can be achieved, inspires us to try for ourselves, and reminds us we do not live in isolation, but community.

Prayer

Jesus, you gave sight to the man born blind, giving him new hope. Use us, your people, to bring your healing and hope to those who are in need. Let us be sensitive to the needs of others; let us consider them before we consider ourselves; let us be tireless in helping; and let all we do be done for the glory and honour of your name. Help those who cannot see your love, witness it in our lives.

Where there is darkness, Lord, let us bring your light.
Where there is despondency, Lord, let us bring new hope.
Where there is suffering, Lord, let us bring your comfort and healing.
That others may come to know you as their loving God. Amen.

Saints Peter and Paul

29 June

Simon, son of Jonas, brother of Andrew, was a fisherman in Capernaum on the Sea of Galilee. Andrew met Jesus first and brought Simon to him. Jesus gave Simon the name Cephas, the Aramaic for the Greek word Petros, which means Rock.

From the beginning Jesus seems to have chosen Peter to be the leader of the Apostles. With James and John, Peter was present at the raising of Jairus' daughter, at the Transfiguration, and apart from the other disciples in the Garden of Gethsemane. At Caesarea Philippi, Peter made his great confession of faith in Jesus, "You are the Christ, the Son of the living God" (Matthew 16:16). Jesus replied, "And I tell you that you are Peter, and on this rock I will build my church, and the gates of hell will not overcome it. I will give you the keys of the kingdom of heaven" (Matthew 16:18-20).

At the Last Supper Jesus predicted that Peter would desert him and deny him. Peter's denials of Jesus are recorded by all four gospel-writers in great detail, which seems to emphasise an event relatively insignificant in the whole of Jesus' passion. They all pay tribute to the importance of Peter in the early Church. In John's gospel Peter is restored to his place with the threefold commission to feed the sheep and lambs of Christ (John 21:15-17).

On Easter Sunday after Mary Magdalene had found the tomb empty Peter and John ran to the sepulchre. John arrived first but did not dare go in; impetuous Peter went straight in. Peter was the first to realise that Jesus was still alive. After the Ascension, Peter took the lead among the disciples in choosing Matthias to replace Judas Iscariot. At Pentecost it was Peter who addressed the crowd. Later he healed a crippled beggar at the Beautiful Gate of the Temple and preached to the crowds and to the Sanhedrin.

Early historians link Peter with Rome and it is said that he was the first Bishop there. We are told that he was condemned to be crucified during the reign of Nero. Tradition has it that Peter asked to be crucified upside down because he was not worthy to die in the same way as Jesus.

Tradition also says that Peter and Paul were executed on the same day. Not together, because Peter was crucified and Paul, as a Roman citizen, was beheaded. It was June 29th A.D. 65. Peter's body was moved from the cemetery in the Appian Way to its final resting-place under the high altar of St Peter's in the Vatican.

St Peter is a very popular saint, not only because he was important but because he is so human. He was outspoken, he was impulsive and impetuous. He could be brave: he stood up before the Sanhedrin; yet he could also be a coward: he ran away from Gethsemane; he denied Jesus three times; he was prepared to change his mind about Gentiles in the Church. He made mistakes, but he always tried to make amends for them. You can recognise pictures of St Peter by the keys he carries, by a cockerel, signifying his denial, or by an upside-down cross.

Thought

Peter and Paul, each in his own right, were powerful proclaimers of the Good News of Jesus Christ; together, they show something more. Different personalities, different temperaments, different gifts, different weaknesses, all working together for good and for God. Their joint witness shows the power of the Holy Spirit to bring people together; and shows the importance of tolerance, co-operation and mutual respect amongst those who profess the name of Christ.

Prayer

Lord Jesus, you chose ordinary men and women to take your message of life and peace to the world. Peter and Paul were weak, but you turned their weaknesses into strengths, and their lives showed your power. In the same way, Lord, take our weaknesses and transform them, so that we too might be of service to you, and proclaim your Good News.

Turn us from sin, O God, that we might live virtuous lives.
Give us peace in our heart, O God, that we may truly rejoice in you.
Grant us your salvation, O God, that we might bring that same
  salvation to others. Amen.

Martin Niemöller

1 July

Martin Niemöller was born on 14th January 1892 in Lippstadt, the son of a German pastor. Martin became a naval officer and was the commander of a U-boat in the First World War. Although he was a brave man whose life was often in danger, his experiences of the war, the loss of life and the futility of killing, made him turn more to his religion. He became a pastor and in 1931 was given the parish of Dahlem, a fashionable suburb of Berlin.

His bravery was again tested with the coming to power of the Nazis under Adolf Hitler. In 1933 he protested against attempted Nazi interference in church affairs. He set up the Pastor's Emergency League, especially to combat discriminations against Christians of Jewish background. He fought hard against Hitler's efforts to bring the German churches under his control. On 1st July 1937, Martin was arrested by the Gestapo, the secret police. He was tried seven months later – the trial was a mockery – and sent to Sachsenhausen concentration camp. In 1941 he was transferred to another camp at Dachau, and then moved to the Tirol in 1945, where he was freed by Allied forces.

After the Second World War Martin helped to rebuild the Evangelical Church in Germany and he became a leading member of the Bekennede Kirche, the Confessing Church. In 1961 he was elected as one of the six presidents of the World Council of Churches, a position he held until 1968. He became a controversial pacifist, and spoke strongly against the nuclear arms race. He was awarded the Lenin Peace Prize in 1967 and the Grand Cross of Merit, West Germany's highest honour, in 1971. He died in Wiesbaden on 6th March 1984.

Thought

Those who experience violence and warfare first hand, as combatants, observers or victims, make the most convincing promoters of peace.

They know the agony and futility of war. But often, in opposing violence and dedicating themselves to peace, they expose themselves to the violent words and actions of those they wish to convince. Niemöller knew war, yet was able to become a tireless worker for peace, in spite of the cost to himself.

Prayer

Creator God, you made all people to live in harmony and peace, and your Son Jesus came to restore peace to our troubled hearts and our violent world. May the Spirit of Jesus inspire us to witness to peace, at home, at school, wherever we may be. When we desire to hurt, in what we do or say, let us rather show tolerance, forgiveness and a reconciling spirit. Let us work with all who work for your peace. Amen.

You desire all people to live in peace, Lord: help them.
Your way is not the way of violence or hatred, Lord: teach us.
With you, all things are possible, Lord: grant us peace.
Let us learn from the life of Martin Niemöller that peace is always worth
*   seeking, in your name.*
Amen.

St Clare of Assisi

11 August

We live in a materialistic age and we fear poverty. So we find it is difficult to understand people like St Francis and St Clare who embraced poverty completely - taking the words of Jesus "sell all you have and give to the poor" literally. To have nothing liberated Francis and Clare so they could concentrate on spiritual things. Francis described poverty, or "Lady Poverty" as he called it as ".... the way to salvation, the nurse of humility and the root of perfection".

Clare was born in about 1193 in Assisi, Italy. When she was eighteen St Francis preached some Lenten sermons at the church of St George, in Assisi. Clare was so impressed that she decided to follow the way of St Francis.

On Palm Sunday, 1212, Clare went to the Cathedral of Assisi for the blessing of palms. That evening Clare ran away from home and walked a mile out of Assisi to where Francis and his community lived. The brothers met her at the door of the Chapel of Our Lady of the Angels and escorted her inside. There she threw down her jewellery and fine clothes and Francis himself cut off her long hair. She put on a garment made of sackcloth and tied a knotted rope round her waist. She was then taken to a Benedictine convent of nuns.

Her family came to take her home and tried to drag her out of the chapel where she had sought sanctuary. Seeing that she would not change her mind, they left her in the convent. Later she was joined by her sister Agnes, aged fourteen. Later still Clare was joined by her mother and her other sister Beatrice and by sixteen other ladies. They lived in a small house adjoining the chapel of St Damian, which Francis himself had restored. Their rule was inspired by St Francis and they lived in extreme poverty. They wore grey habits with black hoods, ate one meal a day (never meat), and were bare-footed. They tended the sick, sent to them by Francis, and made church linen and embroidered it. Clare was particularly strict on herself and never left her convent. For the last twenty-seven years of her life she suffered various illnesses.

Although often bedridden she spent hours in prayer and also sewed altar cloths and linen for Assisi's churches.

Clare nursed Francis in his last illness, and after he had died in 1226 his body was taken to the convent before being taken for burial so that the nuns could pay their last respects. Two years later, in 1228, Pope Gregory IX came to Assisi to canonise Francis. He tried to get Clare to relax her vows of poverty, but she refused, and the Pope allowed her the right never to be forced to receive possessions.

Clare died on 11th August 1253, and was made a saint two years later by Pope Alexander IV. She was buried in the church of St George, Assisi, but her remains were taken to a new church built in her honour in 1260.

Like the Franciscan friars, the Poor Clares spread all over Europe, in particular Spain, France, Bohemia and England. Like Francis, Clare devoted her whole life to 'Lady Poverty'. She saw Francis imitating Jesus and wanted to follow his example; in doing so, she gave up everything else. She called herself 'The Little Flower of St Francis'.

Thought

Poverty, in itself, is not a virtue. Countless millions of people in the world live in the misery of poverty, and long to escape. St Clare, however, dedicated herself to poverty; for her and for the religious sisters who lived with her, the renouncing of all possessions was a sign of their total dedication to Christ. Nothing would distract her; and in living this voluntary poverty, she was challenging the way of the world, where wealth is importance, and poverty is worthlessness. The religious sisters of Clare, known today as 'Poor Clares', continue this witness.

Prayer

Gentle God, you watch over us with the tenderness of a mother, wishing to bless us with every good thing; help us to know what is important in life, and what has little value. Show us the dignity and worth of every person, that we might treat all with respect. May we seek justice, that all people may have what they need to live. And may the example of Clare prompt us to dedicate ourselves to Christ, who is Lord for ever and ever.

In poverty, Clare gave herself wholly to Christ.
  Lord, make us generous, that others might live.
In simplicity, Clare demonstrated the importance of prayer.
  Lord, help us to pray.
In her hidden life, Clare relied on God's mercy.
  Lord, help us to call on your saving help.
Amen.

Maximilian Kolbe

14 August

Maximilian Kolbe was born on 8th January 1894, at Zdunska Wola, near Lodz, Poland. In a deeply religious country he joined the Franciscan friars in 1907. In 1912 he went to Rome where he studied theology and philosophy at the Pontifical Gregorian University. He was especially devoted to Jesus' mother, Mary, and founded the devotional association of the Militia of Mary Immaculate. In 1918 he was ordained priest and returned to Poland to start a monthly religious paper and a religious centre devoted to the Blessed Virgin Mary. The centre eventually contained some 700 friars and workers. He founded sister institutions in Japan, in 1930 and in India, and then returned to Poland to take charge of the centre there.

In 1939 the Germans invaded Poland, an act which brought Great Britain and France into the Second World War. Maximilian was arrested by the Gestapo, the secret police, but after interrogation was released. In 1941 he was arrested again and charged with helping Jews and the Polish underground movement. He was imprisoned in Warsaw and then sent to the concentration camp at Auschwitz. In July 1941 a prisoner escaped from the camp and the commandant announced that ten prisoners would be killed by being starved to death. Ten men were picked at random and one of them, Franciszek Gajowniczek, pleaded for his life because he had a wife and children. Maximilian stepped forward and asked if he might be allowed to take the man's place. It was agreed and Maximilian joined the other nine in a special cell. He led them in prayers and hymn singing and over the weeks they died one by one until only Maximilian was left. On 14th August 1941, Maximilian was given a lethal injection of phenol and then his body was cremated.

Maximilian's noble act was not forgotten. In 1971 he was beatified and on 10th October 1982, a fellow Pole, Pope John Paul II declared Maximilian to be a saint and martyr.

"No one has greater love than this, to lay down one's life for one's friends" (John 15:13).

Thought

Inner freedom is a precious gift. It enables the person who possesses it to live entirely for others and, if necessary, to die for them too. Inner freedom is a life-time goal: something to which many of us aspire, but very few of us achieve. Maximilian Kolbe was able to offer his life that someone else might live; in this, he showed his freedom, and the courage and strength it gave him. Such freedom is a worthy aspiration, and though it may not be fully attained in this life, each step towards it is blessed.

Prayer

Holy Spirit of God, you blow where you will, entirely free. You speak to our hearts, calling us to be free. Help us to attain that freedom which only you, the God who made us to be free, can give. Like Maximilian Kolbe, let our inner freedom inspire others, give them hope, and help them in turn to be free. Spirit of freedom and Spirit of life, fill us, inspire us and make us free. Amen.

From all that harms us, Lord protect us.
In all that hurts us, Lord, heal us.
From all that binds us, Lord, set us free.
Amen.

Mother Teresa of Calcutta

11 August

The girl who grew up to be known as Mother Teresa was born on 27th August 1910, at Skopje, in Yugoslavia. Her name was Agnes Gonxha Bojaxhiu. Her parents were Albanian and her father ran a grocer's shop. She went to the local school with her brother and sister and at the age of 12 declared that God wanted her to be a nun. At the age of 18 she joined the Irish Order of the Sisters of Loretto, taking the name Teresa after St Teresa of Avila. "That is when my life began," she wrote.

In 1928 she was sent to India to teach at St Mary's High School, Calcutta, a school run by her Order. She took her final vows in 1937 and eventually became the Principal of the School. The School was a privileged one, but outside there were poor, lepers, and dying people, who were being completely ignored. In 1948 Teresa asked for permission to stay in the Order but to leave the Convent to help the poor. Teresa went to work in the slums. She discarded her nun's habit and wore a white sari with a blue border. She had a small cross pinned on her left shoulder, and she wore open sandals. She was soon looking after five destitute children in a friend's flat. Numbers grew and grew, and she was helped by the teachers and girls of her old school.

There was so much to be done. Teresa was given permission to found an order of nuns, the Congregation of the Missionaries of Charity. One day she found an old woman dying in the gutter. She was covered in rubbish and her body was partially eaten by rats and ants. Teresa opened a home for the dying in Calcutta, where people could die with dignity. She also opened 'Shanti Nagar' (Town of Peace), a colony for lepers near Asansol in West Bengal. "What the poor and sick need, is to be wanted. Being unwanted is the worst disease that any human being can experience."

Mother Teresa's order grew, and there were over 60 schools, orphanages and homes for the dying spread over the world. In 1963 she started the Missionary Brothers of Charity. Her good work was recognised in 1971 when she was awarded the Pope John XXIII Peace Prize, and in 1976 when she was awarded the Nobel Peace Prize. She accepted the prizes on behalf of the poor and the money was used to help them. In 1990 with increased ill-health Mother Teresa retired from most active work. She died on 7th September 1997.

Many people saw Mother Teresa as a saint, but that was contrary to her wishes. She saw herself as an instrument of God, as she called it, 'a little pencil in God's hand'.

"We can do no great things, only small ones with great love. God does not mind how much we do, what affects him is how much love we put into the work."

"Mary can teach us kindness. 'They have no wine,' she told Jesus at Cana. Let us, like her, be aware of the needs of the poor, be they spiritual or material, and let us, like her, give generously of the love and grace we are granted.

Thought

Certainly one of the most famous Christians of our day, Mother Teresa owed her prominence to her commitment to those who have no voice, those who might otherwise be entirely overlooked, those for whom there might be no other help. In that, she showed the values of the Reign of God, seeing people as Jesus sees them. To see in this way is to be prophetic, observing what is there, but not visible to the careless passer-by.

Prayer

Jesus, you love all people, regardless of status, disposition or wealth. From you we learn that every person bears the likeness of their Creator, and was made to share God's glory. Help us to love all people in the same way as you do; help us to serve them selflessly, inspired by the selfless dedication of Mother Teresa and countless others; and help us to see your face in all who suffer, that we might bring comfort. Give us the vision and the courage we need to serve you. Amen.

In all we say or do, may we work for a better world.
In all we hope or dream, let us plan for a brighter future.
In all we are, let us rejoice. Amen.

John Bunyan

31 August

John Bunyan was born in 1628 in Elstow, Bedfordshire, the son of a tinker who made and sold pots and pans. John joined the Parliamentary army in 1644 where he came across many different non-conformist groups. He saw little military action and when a comrade took his place at the siege of Leicester and was killed, John thought that he had been saved by divine providence.

After his discharge from the army John married in 1649. His first child, Mary, was blind. His other children were Elizabeth, John and Thomas. In 1653 John joined a group of non-conformists and became a well-known preacher. When King Charles II was restored to the throne the freedom that non-conformists enjoyed was ended. In 1660 John was arrested and imprisoned and spent the next 12 years in gaol. Prison was different for John than it would be today. He was sometimes allowed out to visit family or friends; he preached to other prisoners; and we are told that he made laces and sold them at the prison door to earn money to support his family. In prison he wrote at least six books. In Grace Abounding to the Chief of Sinners, which was published in 1666, John tells of his early life and how he found inner peace, contentment and faith.

After his release from prison in 1672 John became a minister at a Baptist church in Bedford. In 1677 he was again imprisoned for his beliefs. During six months in gaol John Bunyan finished his most famous book, The Pilgrim's Progress. The pilgrim in The Pilgrim's Progress is called Christian. Christian journeys to reach the Celestial City, guided by a man called Evangelist. He has all sorts of adventures, sometimes good, sometimes bad. On the advice of Mr Worldly Wiseman, a pompous snob, he leaves God's path until Evangelist is able to put him back on it. Christian is nearly killed by arrows from Captain Beelzebub's Castle.

He follows the straight and narrow path to a cross, where he prays for God's mercy. The great pack on his back, representing his sins, falls off and rolls away. Other adventures follow. Christian fights the dreadful beast Apollyon and comes to the Valley of the Shadow of Death. He meets Faithful and they go to Vanity Fair, where they are locked up and mocked. They are tried before Lord Hategood and Faithful is tortured and burned. Christian sees him going up to heaven in a horse-drawn chariot. Christian escapes only to be caught by Giant Despair and imprisoned in Doubting Castle. He is freed when he prays and goes to Delectable Mountain, where he meets Atheist. Finally he reaches the river, across which lies the Celestial City.

In 1688 Bunyan rode to Reading to act as peacemaker between a father and son. He then rode on to London in pouring rain, caught a chill and fever and died on 31st August.

Thought

Bodily captivity can allow the spirit to soar free, and for this we can be grateful. Whilst in prison for his beliefs, John Bunyan wrote his 'Pilgrim's Progress', an allegory of the Christian life. Our life may be different from Bunyan's, our path will not be identical to his; but pilgrims we are, with all the vulnerabilities, disappointments, temptations and hopes of a pilgrim's life. We are strengthened by the Lord who walks with us, and who is our journey's end. And when our bodies fail, our spirits can soar free.

Prayer

Journey with us, Lord, every step of the way. When we are lost, show us the way; when we are tired, give us strength; when we are afraid, give us courage; when we are burdened, give us help. May we journey onwards, doing what good we may, confident in the victory of your justice and the tenderness of your mercy. And at the end of our journey, grant us the sweetest rest, with you and all the saints for ever. Amen.

At the beginning of the day, in hope, Lord, I pray, walk with me.
In the heat of the day, in friendship, Lord, I pray, rejoice with me.
In the evening of the day, trustingly, Lord, I pray, remain with me for
  ever. Amen.

The Blessed Virgin Mary

8 September

There are six major feast days in the Church's year for the Blessed Virgin Mary. 2nd February, the Presentation of Christ in the Temple; 25th March, the Annunciation; 2nd July, the Visitation; 15th August, the Assumption; 8th September, the Nativity; 8th December, the Conception.

The Church owes a great debt of love and devotion to Mary. We are told that she belonged to the house of David. Tradition says that her parents were called Joachim and Anne. She obviously figures prominently in the infancy stories of Jesus found in the gospels according to Luke and Matthew. Luke gives the story of the annunciation by the angel Gabriel; the visit to Elizabeth; the birth at Bethlehem; and the coming of the shepherds. He describes Mary's purification, when Jesus was presented to God, and later when Jesus was found in the temple, Luke 2:41-52.

Matthew records the message of the angel to Joseph, the coming of the wise men and the escape to Egypt. Luke gives the story from Mary's point of view; Matthew gives more prominence to Joseph. Both gospels state clearly that Jesus' birth was miraculous; that the second person of the Holy Trinity became human by the power of the Holy Spirit in Mary's womb.

St John tells us of the wedding feast at Cana in Galilee. Mary said to Jesus, "They have no wine left." She told the servants to do anything Jesus commanded. When Jesus was on the cross he commended his mother to the care of St John, so presumably from then on she lived with John.

Mary is not mentioned as having seen Jesus after his resurrection but tradition says that he appeared to her first of all. In the Acts of the Apostles Mary was with the disciples and received the Holy Spirit with them on that first Pentecost. Mary did not go about preaching, she remained in the background supporting the apostles with her prayers.

One tradition claims that Mary died in Jerusalem, another that she went to Ephesus with St John and died there. The Feast of the Assumption on 15th August is the traditional date for her falling asleep. A legend says that when the apostles opened her tomb it was found empty except for lilies and roses. In 1950 Pope Pius XII defined it as an article of faith that at the end of her earthly life Mary was taken up body and soul to heaven.

In the year 431 the Council of Ephesus gave Mary the title of Theotokos, a Greek word meaning God-bearer. We usually translate the word as Mother of God. The Council of Trent in 1547 declared that Mary was free of original sin. The Church believes that both before and after the birth of Jesus Mary was a virgin and remained so.

The Thirty-nine Articles of the Church of England forbid the invocation of saints, including Mary, but in recent times many Anglicans have adopted a position no different from Roman Catholics. In the eastern churches there has always been a deep respect and veneration of the Blessed Virgin. However we each understand the role Mary played in the life of Jesus, it is our Christian duty to honour and respect her.

Thought

The mother of Jesus is honoured by many Christians for her co-operation with God, through which Jesus was born; she is honoured for the example of her life, how she responded in faith to the ministry of her Son; and she is honoured for her place in the whole mystery of our salvation. Everything that touches Christ, in a sense, becomes sacred. We celebrate the birth of Mary as another happy chapter in the history of our redemption, giving glory to God for all that God has done.

Prayer

Lord Jesus Christ, we honour Mary your mother for her faithfulness, her courage and her love. Nurture in our hearts the grace that filled hers, that we too might give you to the world. Let us ponder the mysteries of your life as she pondered them; like her, rejoicing in the goodness and mercy of God. And let us, like her, be welcomed into the glory of heaven, saved by your grace. Amen.

As people of faith, let us glorify the Lord for the wonder of creation.
As people of hope, let us look forward to the salvation of the world.
As people of love, let us nurture goodness in all people,
    that the Reign of God may come. Amen.

St Vincent de Paul

27 September

Vincent de Paul was born in about 1580 in a village in the south of France. His parents had a small farm and Vincent used to look after the sheep when he was a boy. After studying at Toulouse, Vincent was ordained priest in 1600 and became one of the chaplains to Queen Margaret of Valois. Vincent was captured by pirates in 1605 and taken to Tunis in North Africa, where he was a slave for two years before escaping.

In 1609 Vincent met a holy priest, Pierre de Berulle, in Paris. Pierre found Vincent a post as tutor to the children of the Count de Gondi, who was in charge of the galleys. In those days, instead of being sent to prison, some people who were convicted of crimes were sentenced to the cruel punishment of being galley slaves in ships. Vincent had pity on them and worked hard to improve their conditions. When he later became a parish priest he continued his work with the poor and the oppressed, and this was to be his work for the rest of his life.

In 1625 Vincent founded a community of priests who devoted themselves to working in the smaller towns and villages. They were given the name Congregation of the Mission, but were also known as Lazarists, from the name of their church of St Lazare; or Vincentians, after Vincent himself.

In 1633 Vincent founded, together with (St) Louise de Marillac, the Sisters of Charity, who were the first group of sisters to go about among the poor and sick to offer them help and healing. Previously, orders of nuns had to stay in their convents. Sister Louise made the order a great success, especially providing hospital care for the poor. Vincent persuaded rich people to collect funds, to visit hospitals, to organise relief for the needs of the poor and to help educate them.

Vincent also founded a hospital for abandoned babies. In Paris, each year some three to four hundred babies were left to die in the streets. It is said that night after night he wandered about the slums of Paris looking for abandoned infants. He wrapped them up in his cloak and brought them back to his hospital.

During the wars in Lorraine, on the border between France and Germany, Vincent collected money in Paris to send to the war victims. He sent missionaries to the poor and suffering in Poland, Ireland and Scotland. He ransomed over 1200 Christian slaves in North Africa.

Vincent became a legend in his own lifetime. His charity was boundless. Clergy and laity, rich and poor, convicts and galley slaves were all helped by a man who devoted his life to others for the love of Jesus.

Towards the end of his life Vincent suffered from serious ill health. On 27th September 1660, he died peacefully while sitting in his chair. He was eighty years old. The peasant priest, Vincent, was declared a saint by Pope Clement XII in 1737. Vincent is the patron saint of all charitable societies.

Thought

The religious life of Jesus was not spent primarily in the synagogue or Temple, but in the countryside and in the street. Jesus went out to people, not staying at home waiting for them to come to him. His urgent mission meant he sought out the lost and the sick bringing his healing and hope. St Vincent de Paul rediscovered this urgent mission of Jesus, and lived it tirelessly. He is a sign of the love of God made flesh, Good News by what he said and did, and what others say and do, to this day, in his name.

Prayer

Lord, the hungry look not for reassurance, but for bread; the sick look not for mere words, but for comfort; the lost look not for advice, but reassurance. You brought to each person what they most needed, and you charge us to do the same in your name. Like Vincent, let us seek to serve you in our daily life, and come together to praise you and ask you for help.

When we pray, Lord, inspire us to do your work.
When we do your work, Lord, help us to pray.
In all things, Lord, be with us, that we may do your will and live to give
you glory. Amen.

Harvest Festival

When a boy was asked by his teacher where his food came from he answered, "Tesco." Which is, of course, the right answer, but not the only one. Ask, "How did it get to Tesco?" and the answer is still easy, "By lorry, from the depot." Ask, "But where did it come from originally?" then the answer needs a bit more thought.

Let's say you had a big breakfast today. If you had tea to drink it might have come from India, Kenya, Sri Lanka, China. If you had coffee, it could have been grown in Africa or South America. The cereal for your cornflakes or muesli could have been grown in the United States, Canada, or Britain. The same for the wheat in your bread. Milk might be from local cows, the sugar from the Caribbean. Your orange juice could have been made from oranges grown in Spain, Israel, South America, or South Africa. The butter on your toast might have come from New Zealand, your eggs from the farm down the road and your bacon from Denmark. And the bar of Swiss chocolate you put aside for your morning break is made from cocoa beans grown in West Africa.

Harvest festival is the time to thank God for all the good things that the earth gives for our enjoyment as well as to keep us alive. A good harvest means we won't go hungry, but some of the people who grow food for us don't have enough for themselves. About forty million people die of starvation every year and fifteen million of them are children. Seventy per cent of the grain in the world is eaten by the richest twenty per cent of the world's population. When you boiled the kettle for your tea or coffee you got the water from the tap; in some parts of the world there is no clean water at all. Each year twenty-five million people die from water-related diseases.

In the Lord's prayer we say, "give us this day our daily bread." We don't say, "give me," but, "give us." And the word bread means not just bread but all the things we need. So, being grateful to God at Harvest Festival means also being grateful to the people who have grown, made, handled, transported, the good things we have. The simplest way of showing our gratitude would be to pray for all these people.

An atlas can be a very useful prayer book. Younger children could turn a page each day and pray for the people in the countries on that page. Older children might like to listen to the news and pray for people in countries facing war, famine, disaster and disease.

Thought

'Harvest', in the strictly agricultural sense, means little to most people in our urbanised society. But we celebrate the fruits of the earth, given us that we might live; and we celebrate the fruits of human labour, all that we produce through our work. In work, as in recreation and in rest, we are engaging in something human, something necessary for life, and something which is a gift from God. Let us give thanks for the 'fruit of the earth, the work of human hands' (from the Prayers over the Gifts of the Mass).

Prayer

Blessed are you, Lord, God of all creation. You created heaven and earth, you bless us with life, you give nourishment and growth. Give us grateful hearts, that we might thank you for your goodness; deepen our respect for our world, that we may not damage or destroy what is good; let us share the resources of our planet justly, that all might have what they need to live; and let us work well, enjoying the fruits of our labours. Through Christ our Lord. Amen.

You made heaven and earth, Lord, and said it was good.
You created plants and creatures,
    and gave them life,
    and that was good too.
You made man and woman from the dust of earth,
    making them stewards of your creation,
    and that was good.
Help us to live in your goodness,
    according to your will. Amen.

St Thérèse of Lisieux

3 October

Marie Françoise-Thérèse Martin was born in 1873 at Alençon, France, the youngest of five daughters who all became nuns. Her mother died when she was four years old and her father moved to Lisieux where his children might be closer to their uncle and aunt.

When Thérèse was nine her sister Pauline entered the Carmelite convent in Lisieux. When Thérèse was nearly fourteen her sister Marie joined the Carmelites also. Thérèse wanted to enter the convent as well but she was too young. She was determined, and when on a visit to Rome with her father, at a public audience with the Pope, Thérèse spoke up boldly and asked him to let her enter Carmel at fifteen. Leo XIII was impressed with her determination but left the decision to Thérèsa's bishop. In April 1888 Thérèse entered Carmel, three months after her fifteenth birthday.

Although delicate Thérèse carried out all the practices of the austere Carmelite rule, except that she was not allowed to fast, she carried out the Carmelite duty of praying for priests with great fervour. Thérèse volunteered to do missionary work in Vietnam, but on the night of Maundy Thursday 1895, she began to bleed at the mouth, the first sign of the tuberculosis that was to kill her. The last eighteen months of her life was a time of great suffering. In June 1897 she was moved to the convent infirmary where she remained until her death on 30th September 1897. She was only twenty-four years old. Thérèse would probably have died unknown if her Superior had not ordered her to keep a diary. It was published after her death and became popular with Christians and non-Christians alike. The Story of a Soul was a spectacular success and a number of miracles and favours were attributed to her heavenly prayers. Pope Pius XI beatified her in 1923 and declared her a saint in 1925.

In the convent Thérèsa's life was simple, unselfish and obedient. Thinking about her approaching death she wrote that after it, "I will let fall a shower of roses," meaning favours and miracles through her intercession. Because of this she is familiarly known as the Little Flower. She is not only a patron saint of missions and a co-patron of France, she is the patron saint of florists.

Her favourite flowers were roses and at her canonisation in 1925, St Peter's in Rome was decorated with red roses. As Pius XI declared her a saint a handful of red petals from above the pope's chair fell gently to the ground near his feet.

Thérèse is often pictured in her Carmelite habit, holding a bunch of roses. She spoke of her life as "the way of spiritual childhood, the way of trust and absolute surrender".

Thought

Through her 'Little Way', Thérèse wished to attain holiness through the challenges and trials of everyday life. Everything that happened, she said, could be a means of grace. This approach to life is profoundly sacramental: every person and every situation offering an encounter with Jesus Christ. There is no need to seek Jesus in the extraordinary, when he is all around us in the ordinary. Our meeting with him every day is what saves us.

Prayer

O God, give us the grace to serve you in the ordinary things in life. What we do, help us to do well; what we say, let it be for the encouragement of others; what we think, may it be from selfless hearts. Let us find holiness in living our lives as best we can, with your help. Like Thérèse, may we keep your goodness in mind, and serve you with grateful hearts. We ask this through Jesus Christ our Lord. Amen.

We do not ask to be heroes, Lord, but to live our daily lives well.
We do not ask for fame, but to be known as your people.
We do not ask for reward, but only to know we have given you service,
    thanks and praise.
Amen.

St Francis of Assisi

4 October

Francis was born in Assisi, Umbria, in about 1181. His father was a prosperous cloth merchant. As a young man Francis had plenty of money and spent it lavishly. He trained as a soldier and in a battle against the nearby town of Perugia was captured and imprisoned for a year. When he was released he became seriously ill. After his recovery Francis was out riding and met a leper who was terribly disfigured. The leper begged for alms but Francis ignored him and rode by. Then he had second thoughts and turned back. He gave the leper all the money he had and then kissed him.

One day Francis entered the ruined chapel of St Damian near Assisi. While he was praying he heard a voice coming from the crucifix, "Go and repair my house, which you see is falling down." Francis assumed that the chapel had to be repaired, so he took a load of cloth from his father's warehouse and sold it. He took the money to the poor priest of St Damian's who refused it; Francis left the money on the window ledge.

Francis' father was very angry, found his son, dragged him home and beat him. Francis was summoned before the bishop and was told to return the money to his father. Francis did as he was told and added, "The clothes I wear are also his." He took them off and gave them to his father. One of the bishop's servants gave Francis an old cloak.

For two years Francis wandered as a hermit, telling people about the love of Jesus Christ. Many people admired Francis and some joined him. Their numbers increased. They preached, cared for the sick, especially lepers and begged their food. Their most distinctive mark was their happiness and they were called Joculatores Domini, the Lord's clowns. In 1210 Francis and his brothers went to Rome to ask the Pope's approval for their way of life.

The new Franciscan order grew rapidly and spread across Europe. In 1219 Francis went to Egypt where the crusaders were fighting the Saracens. He managed to pass through the Saracen lines and was brought before the Sultan, who listened to Francis but was not converted. When Francis returned to Italy he let other friars take charge of the administration of the order. He spent Christmas of 1223 at the village of Greccio, where he made the first crib. In 1224 he spent some time on the mountain retreat of La Verna, where, in prayer, he received the marks of the wounds of Jesus in his hands, feet and side.

During the last two years of his life Francis was in pain from these wounds and he slowly went blind. He visited his friend St Clare at her convent and wrote his Canticle of Brother Sun. We sing a version of it today in the hymn, All creatures of our God and King.

Francis returned to Assisi to die. As he lay dying he took bread and broke it and gave some to everyone present as a sign of love and peace. "I have done my part, may Christ teach you to do yours," he said. In the evening of 3rd October 1226 Francis died. He was forty-five years old.

Thought

Francis wrought a revolution in the Church and in the society of his day. He cut through centuries of ecclesiastical complexity to rediscover the simplicity of the Gospel of Christ. In him, in his way of life, and in the brotherhood he founded, Francis challenged an institutional church that had, in many respects, lost sight of the vision of Jesus. His radical discipleship was a reminder to many not to lose sight of the Good News, and constantly seek spiritual renewal rather than simply do things 'the way they have always been done'. The Franciscan spirit is a necessary challenge to the Church to this present day.

Prayer

Lord Jesus, you came to proclaim the Reign of God, and allowed nothing to stand in the way of your mission. Like Francis, help us to be single-minded in our discipleship; help us to rejoice in creation, and help us to be tolerant of those whose opinions differ from our own. Help us to be mindful that we are stewards of creation, and to use the resources around us wisely and justly. We ask this in your name, Amen.

Make us instruments, Lord of your peace, this day and every day.
May we proclaim your Good News in word and in deed.
Renew the whole of creation, that all might give glory to you. Amen.

Edith Cavell

12 October

Edith Louise Cavell came from Swardeston in Norfolk, where she was born in 1865. Edith trained as a governess and eventually went to Brussels to look after the children of a Belgian lawyer. When she was 29 she returned home to look after her sick father. It was then that she decided to become a nurse.

Edith trained in various London hospitals and became assistant matron at Shoreditch. In 1907 she returned to Brussels as matron of the first training school for nurses in Belgium. In 1914 the First World War began and Belgium was occupied by German forces. The training school became a Red Cross hospital that cared for German patients as well as allied troops. Edith was involved with an underground group which helped wounded and sick British, French and Belgian soldiers to reach the Netherlands, a neutral country.

On 5th August 1915 Edith and several others were arrested. She was kept in solitary confinement and in her cell all she had was a folding bed, a stool, a cupboard and a jug of water. She was allowed half an hour of exercise twice a week. To pass the time she read The Imitation of Christ by Thomas Kempis and did embroidery.

Her court martial began on 7th October. The charge read that over 250 soldiers had reached Holland through her efforts, but Edith insisted that her sole concern was to help the wounded to be healed and set free on humanitarian grounds. On 11th October she was condemned to death with four others. That night, the last night of her life, she was visited by Stirling Graham, a Church of England minister. She took Holy Communion, recited the hymn 'Abide with me' and talked with Graham.

"I am glad to give my life rather than any of my soldiers should have fallen into the hands of the Germans," she said. "I have no fear. I have seen death so often that it is not strange to me. Life has always been hurried. This time of rest has been a great mercy. Everyone here has been very kind. This I would say, standing as I do in view of God and eternity. I realise that patriotism is not enough; I must have no hatred or bitterness towards anyone." Mr Graham said to her, "We shall always remember you as a heroine and as a martyr." Edith replied, "Think of me only as a nurse who tried to do her duty."

Just before six o'clock in the morning of 12th October Edith was taken with Phillipe Baucq, a member of the resistance, to be executed by firing squad. An angry reaction to the killing spread round the world. The others who had been condemned to death had their sentences commuted to imprisonment.

After the end of the war in 1918, Edith's body was brought back to England and buried with full military honours in the shadow of Norwich Cathedral. A monument was erected to her memory near Trafalgar Square in London and bears the inscription, "Patriotism is not enough. I must have no hatred or bitterness towards anyone."

Thought

Events in the world at large sometimes show ordinary behaviour to be truly extraordinary. Edith Cavell was a nurse, dedicated to her profession, desiring to comfort and to heal. Wartime circumstances meant that her work was seen as resisting occupying forces, and so she was condemned to death. In the face of death, she was determined to show no hatred or bitterness to those who would execute her. Doing what she had always done, in an ordinary way, showed the tremendous resilience of the human spirit. If we can do what is ordinary and what is right, whatever the circumstances, we will achieve greatness.

Prayer

Each and every day, Lord, let us wake up with a determination to achieve great things, by just doing what is ordinary and what is right. Let us not see ourselves as heroes or heroines, but as people who believe there is a better way than selfishness, hatred and intolerance. The Gospel calls us to greatness, according to the standards of your Kingdom, Lord; help us to attain that greatness, through your grace. Amen.

What do you want of us, Lord? Tell us, that we may follow your will.
What do you want us to say, Lord? Put your words into our mouths.
Where would you have us go, Lord? Let us follow in your steps. Amen.

All Saints

1 November

If someone says the word "saint", what comes to your mind? Some particular saint, perhaps, one whom you admire? There are so many to choose from, so let us pick three well known saints. St Francis of Assisi, a man who literally gave up everything to follow Jesus and who inspired his friars to do so much good. St Peter, leader of the apostles and who received the keys of the kingdom of heaven. St Paul, who tirelessly travelled to share the good news of Jesus. Both Peter and Paul were put to death for their faith.

Yet all these saints were sinners, and would be the first to admit it. Francis had a temper, Peter denied Jesus, and Paul could be boastful or feel sorry for himself. None of them was perfect. Paul Tillich, a Lutheran theologian who died in 1965, wrote, "The saint is a saint, not because he is good but because he is transparent for something that is more than he himself is." Paul Tillich uses the word 'he', but he could just as well have written 'she'. Saints are men and women and boys and girls in whom Jesus lives and who try to do only what he wants because they love him. In turn they make it easier for us to trust in God because we see his love at work in them. God shines through a saint's life as light shines through a stained glass window.

Where did we get our faith from? It is of course a gift from God but it is supported and strengthened from the example of other people. Perhaps our parents, family, friends; our teachers, godparents, clergy; in fact anyone who tries to live by faith and is a witness to it. None of them is perfect, but that does not deny the validity of their message. And, of course, there will be people looking to us to find God at work in us.

On All Saints Day we remember that every saint is our brother and sister in Jesus. We give thanks to God for all of them, those on earth and those in heaven. We remember the well known saints who have their special days, but there are not enough days in the year to remember the countless other saints who remained faithful to their God, some to the point of giving their lives for Christ. They have passed their message on and have their reward. By the grace of God we try to follow their example so that we may be witnesses to those who follow us.

Thought

Somewhere there is a book with the names of all the saints who ever have been and who ever will be, and our names are written in that book. The book is no ordinary book such a book never could be; it is rather a tribute to the incredible mercy and saving power of God. Knowing that our names are written in that book is no excuse for complacency, but rather an incentive to finish the race we have started, to co-operate with the Lord in the salvation of all the world. Such is a life of glory.

Prayer

Your Holy Spirit living within us, makes us holy, Lord. May your Spirit so fill our lives that we become reflections of your goodness and love, that those seeing us, may glimpse you. As you call us to be saints here on earth, so you make us perfect in heaven. We have before us your promise of salvation and eternal life. For all your goodness, we give you praise. For all your love, we love you in return. Amen.

The saints on earth rely on your grace, O Lord, each day of their lives.
The saints in heaven have been perfected by your grace, O Lord, and
    rejoice.
The saints yet to come will sing your praises, O Lord.
All your saints will gather round your throne in your glory. Count us
    amongst them, by your mercy. Amen.

Remembrance Sunday

Remembrance Sunday is the Sunday closest to the 11th November each year. It was at 11a.m. on the 11th day of the 11th month in 1918 that the guns stopped firing after four years of fighting in the First World War. There had never been war on such a scale before. On the allied side, the side of Britain and France, over five million soldiers died and 13 million were wounded. On the German side about eight and a half million soldiers died and over 21 million were wounded.

The families left behind had to bear the enormous shock and sadness of this terrible loss. The sorrow of so many individuals, families and communities came to be expressed in a national day of remembrance. This became a yearly event. But all that was a very long time ago. Even the Second World War is vague history for many people. What is the point of remembering it all now? The slaughter in the First World War was on such a scale and so horrific that people called it the War to End all Wars, yet twenty years later the world was at war again. Whatever our age, the way we live today has been shaped by these wars. What freedoms we have were bought by the people who risked their lives and by those who died in these wars.

Remembrance may mean different things to different people. Those who took part in war, who lost members of their family or friends, or who still live with their injuries, have their own experiences to remember. What might people who are too young to have experienced war think about? Perhaps sadness at the destruction of young lives like their own, full of eagerness and promise. Gratitude for bravery, self-sacrifice, and for the relative peace we enjoy. Anger that we can be so arrogant, stubborn, and stupid as to kill one another instead of trying to resolve our differences peaceably. Sorrow for the evil of war and that we fall so far short of what Jesus commands us, "Love one another as I have loved you." John 15:12.

The two minutes' silence on Remembrance Sunday could be a time of prayer for peace everywhere in the world. A time to ask Jesus to soften hard hearts with his Holy Spirit of love. A time to pray that leaders of nations and governments will seek the way of peace and justice. A time of gratitude for the sacrifice of all who have given their lives for us, and that we will not be so stupid as to lose all they have gained for us. A time to look at ourselves and see how peaceable we are.

The poppy has become a symbol of Remembrance Sunday. In northern France and Belgium, where much of the First World War was fought, during the spring and summer the fields were carpeted with red poppies which even grew over the battlefield. Soldiers associated the countless flowers with the untold numbers of their dead comrades. After the war poppies were worn as a sign of remembrance and were sold to raise money to help needy ex-servicemen and their families. Today artificial poppies are made in a factory at Richmond in Surrey which produces about 45 million poppies and 70,000 wreaths a year.

Thought

Remembering is at the heart of Christian life; we learn who we are and where we come from by hearing the story of creation, the history of God's people, and the witnesses to Christ's life, death and risen life. This day, we remember the sacrifice of the millions who gave their life that others might live. We remember, and in remembering, honour them; in honouring them, we treasure the freedom they fought to preserve.

Prayer

Father, in your mercy grant eternal rest to all who have died defending freedom; bless all who selflessly give their lives for others; look kindly on all who are victims of aggression, violence and warfare, giving them comfort and hope. Let our solemn remembrance remind us of the horrors of war, the precious gift of peace, and the sacrifices people make for each other. Lord, may we remember, and never forget. We ask this in the name of Jesus your Son, the Prince of Peace. Amen.

Be with those who give their lives for others, Lord, and receive them into your Kingdom.

Grant courage to those who stand up for what is right, and help them persevere to the end.

Inspire us to fight injustice, wherever it may be found, that your people may live in peace. Amen.

St Margaret of Scotland

16 November

Margaret was the granddaughter of the English King Edmund Ironside and was born about the year 1045. Margaret and her children had to flee to Scotland after the Battle of Hastings. They took refuge in the court of King Malcolm III and were joined there by Margaret's younger brother, Edgar.

Margaret was a widow and was intelligent, beautiful, kind and devout. In 1069 Malcolm and Margaret married. They were very happy and had eight children, two of whom, Alexander and David, became Kings of Scotland. Her daughter Matilda married Henry I of England. Through Margaret and Matilda the English royal family can trace their family tree back to pre-Conquest times.

As a devout Christian Margaret took a keen interest in the church in Scotland, then at a low ebb. She encouraged synods which ordered the practice of Easter communion, and the avoidance of servile work on Sundays. She revived the abbey of Iona and built Dunfermline Abbey as a burial-place for the royal family. Her strong English influence was both praised and criticised.

Margaret spent a long time in prayer every day, read holy books and gave much money to the poor. Malcolm could not read and was not especially religious, but he came to respect and value the things his wife believed in. Margaret's biographer, Turgot, prior of Durham and bishop of St Andrew's wrote, "He saw that Christ truly dwelt in her heart … what she rejected, he rejected … what she loved, he, for love of her, loved too."

In 1093, during his fifth invasion of England, Malcolm and one of his sons were killed in a skirmish near Alnwick. Worn out by her austerities and child-bearing, and the added grief of the ·death of Malcolm, Margaret died on 16th November 1093, in Edinburgh. She was buried by the side of her husband in Dunfermline.

Margaret was canonised in 1250. At the Reformation both

Margaret's and Malcolm's bodies were taken to a Chapel in the Escorial, Madrid, which had been built for that purpose.

Thought

Margaret was a wife, a mother and a woman of great faith, piety and devotion. The demands of her everyday life did not keep her from prayer, nor from setting an example to the whole of the royal court, as to how one could serve God, even when exiled from home and living a busy, involved life. And that is the modern challenge: to be immersed in the world, but not to be of the world; to live amongst others, but not to automatically live their values; rather look to God, and the values of God's Reign.

Prayer

Lord, there's often so much we have to fit in to each and every day, and it's hard to find time to pray. It's the one thing we can postpone and postpone, until it hardly happens at all. We wonder, Lord, how we managed to get into this situation. But you understand, Lord. Your Holy Spirit prays in us constantly, enabling us to cry out to you, assuring us that you hear our prayers, encouraging us in all we do. Renew in us, Lord, your spirit of prayer, that we may come to know you more closely. Through Christ our Lord. Amen.

The Lord is close, even when we do not pause to pray.
The Lord listens, even when we do not voice our prayers aloud.
The Lord answers prayer, even when we have lost all hope.
The Lord is God, and is good. Amen.

Catherine of Alexandria

25 November

Catherine is probably the only saint to be remembered today by having a firework named after her.

The stories about Catherine are mostly legend but it is said that she belonged to a noble family in Alexandria, Egypt, in the early fourth century. She devoted herself to study and eventually learnt about Christianity. After a vision of the Virgin Mary and the Child Jesus she was converted. The Emperor Maxentius began persecuting Christians. Catherine went before him and rebuked him. He could not answer her arguments so he summoned fifty philosophers to debate with her. She convinced the philosophers and they all became Christians. The furious Emperor had them burnt to death.

Catherine was eighteen years old and beautiful. Maxentius tried to seduce her and offered her a consort's crown. She refused, saying, "I have surrendered myself as a bride to Christ." Maxentius had her scourged and imprisoned. The Empress was so impressed with Catherine's witness that she, too, became a Christian.

Two hundred of the emperor's soldiers were also converted. Maxentius had them all beheaded and decreed that Catherine should be killed on a spiked wheel. When she was tied to the wheel it said that her bonds were miraculously loosened and the wheel broke in pieces, many of the spikes killing onlookers. Catherine was then taken to be beheaded. Her last words were, "O, hope and salvation of believers, O honour and glory of maidens, Jesus, perfect King, have mercy on me."

Christians in the East began to honour Catherine in the ninth century, and the crusaders brought her story to the West where her popularity grew and grew. In England, 62 churches were dedicated to her and 170 medieval bells still bear her name. Many public houses carry her name. So popular did she become that her day was a public holiday in the Middle Ages.

Catherine is the patron saint of philosophers and philosophy; of learning and students, especially women students; of librarians and libraries, (there was a famous library in Alexandria); of all craftsmen whose work was based on the wheel, such as wheelwrights, spinners and millers.

The story of Catherine is probably a mixture of the lives of several people, but it does tell us that many people have had the courage to die for their faith. Their sacrifice has inspired others when they have faced adversity. We need to remember that even today, some people give up everything, even their lives, because they are Christian. Pray for them, and remember that Catherine is the symbol of them all.

Thought

The blood of martyrs is the seed of the Church, proved by the life and death of Catherine of Alexandria. Her courage and devotion in extreme conditions brought many to faith in Christ. She may have been tempted to renounce her faith, reasoning that if she lived longer, she might be able to do more good; but she resisted, and her faithfulness achieved so much for God. Faithfulness is a sign of the presence of the Holy Spirit of God.

Prayer

We can use reason, Lord, to justify anything we do and appease our conscience; but that is not the way of your truth. Let us be like Catherine, discerning what is right, and allowing nothing to deter us from it. Give us moral courage, determination and strength, that when we face opposition we might overcome it, when others would persuade us to go against your will. And help us to understand your teachings, that we may give true assent. Amen.

When we do not know what to do, show us the way, Lord.
When we do not know the way, guide us, Lord.
When our strength begins to fail, help us, Lord.
Now and every day. Amen.

St Andrew

30 November

St Andrew was the first apostle to be called by Jesus and was the brother of Simon Peter. They had a house in Capernaum on the shore of the Sea of Galilee, where Jesus stayed when he preached in that town. Andrew is named with Peter among the first four in all the biblical lists of the apostles.

At the feeding of the five thousand it was Andrew who told Jesus of the boy with the barley loaves and fish (John 6:8-9). When some Greeks wished to see Jesus they went to Philip, who told Andrew, and the two went to Jesus (John 12:20-22).

It is not known with certainty where Andrew preached the gospel, nor where he died or was buried. He is said to have preached in Scythia, on the northern shores of the Black Sea, and also in Greece. Tradition says that he was arrested in Achaia, in Greece, where it is said that he filled the country with churches and converted the people. In Patras, the Roman proconsul, whose wife had been converted, had Andrew scourged and then tied to a cross so that he might die slowly. The story says that Andrew preached to twenty thousand men for two days before he died. His hearers said, "This holy and debonair man ought not to suffer this," and many became Christians. The idea that Andrew's cross was X-shaped was apparently not known commonly before the fourteenth century.

Under the Emperor Constantine II, who died in 361, St Andrew's relics were taken from Patras to the church of the Apostles in Constantinople. When the crusaders captured Constantinople in 1204 they gave St Andrew's body to Amalfi Cathedral in Italy and his head to Rome. Pope Paul VI returned the head to Constantinople in the 1960s.

What has St Andrew to do with Scotland? Legend says that St Regulus, who was a native of Patras in the fourth century, and was in charge of the relics of St Andrew, was told in a dream by an angel to take some of the relics to an unknown destination. Regulus travelled until the angel told him to stop in Fife, Scotland, and there he built a church which housed the saint's relics. The place was later known as St Andrew's. St Regulus is said to have been helped by King Hung, identified with King Angus MacFergus, an historical character, and the traditional founder of St Andrews. This is how St Andrew came to be the patron saint of Scotland.

St Andrew is also one of the patron saints of Russia, because yet another tradition says that he went to preach the gospel in Kiev, in what is now the Ukraine.

In art Andrew is sometimes shown with an ordinary Latin cross, sometimes with a saltire, or diagonal cross, and sometimes with a net. The flag of Scotland is a saltire cross on a blue background; blue reminding us of the sea and that Andrew was a fisherman.

Thought

Andrew was a manual labourer, a subsistence worker, catching just enough fish to sustain him from day to day. Jesus' choice of such a man to be an apostle is significant: the Gospel was not just for the cultured and sophisticated, but for all; the Gospel is not merely about sitting and learning, but about 'fishing for people'; and each and every person, regardless of social standing, is worthy of the attention of Jesus. Whoever we are, whatever we do or want to achieve, the Lord calls us to serve.

Prayer

Lord, you call us as you called Andrew, challenging us to serve you and to serve our neighbour. Often your call does not involve us leaving our daily life behind, but sometimes it is a challenge to a new way of life. However you call us, wherever you call us, help us to live up to our call. Help us to achieve our full potential as human beings and as your apostles, for in this lies our true peace. Amen.

Today, I will try to speak of the Lord three times, giving thanks and praise.
Today, I will show respect to my neighbour: the Lord expects no less.
Today, I will work well, using the gifts I have been given
In all, I will give glory to God. Amen.

Advent

The word Advent comes from the Latin 'adventus', the coming (of Jesus Christ). In other words we are preparing for the coming of Jesus, but in two different ways: firstly, Jesus coming as a baby at Christmas; secondly, Jesus coming in glory to judge the world on the last day. It is easier to understand the first idea than the second.

In the rush to Christmas the season of Advent can get overlooked. Advent calendars and the Advent wreath can help remind us that these few short weeks sum up centuries of longing and hope that God would send a saviour to his faithful people. Advent is a solemn time, rather like the time of Lent which prepares for Easter.

Many churches have an Advent wreath. It may be made of evergreen, perhaps of interwoven holly and ivy, and it has five candles. Sometimes there are four purple ones round a white candle in the centre. One purple candle is lit on Advent Sunday, the next Sunday two candles are lit, the next Sunday three, and the last Sunday all four. The white candle is lit on Christmas Day. Sometimes there are three purple candles and a pink one. The pink candle is lit on the third Sunday, Rejoice Sunday, which gets its name from the opening verses of the mass of the day. The priest may also wear pink vestments instead of purple. It is though the Church cannot conceal its joy any longer that Jesus is to come at Christmas. Wreaths were used long before Jesus was born, but the Church took those symbols and gave them a deeper meaning. The circle is a symbol of eternity; a circle has no beginning or end. Evergreens, too, point to eternity; they do not die like deciduous leaves. The candles remind us that Jesus is the light of the world and that all Christians are his lights in the world.

Each time we are at mass, just after the Lord's prayer we hear the priest say, "…keep us free from sin and protect us from all anxiety as we wait in joyful hope for the coming of our Saviour, Jesus Christ." We reply, "For the kingdom, the power and the glory are yours, now and for ever." Advent gives us a time to think and pray more deeply about this second coming of Jesus, with joy and with hope. We do not know when that may be, tomorrow or a thousand years away. We hope for things that have not yet happened. Jesus promised he would return and when he does he will gather all things to himself. He will come as the loving judge. The judging part should make us think about ourselves; how much we love him and do what he asks of us, but we should not be frightened. Most of the apostles kept well out of the way when Jesus was arrested and crucified; they ran away. Peter denied him. They had little to feel good about themselves when Jesus appeared to them after rising from the dead. But he said, "Peace be with you," and they were filled with joy. He knew they loved him despite their weaknesses. He loved them, weaknesses and all.

Thought

Waiting expectantly for the coming of the Lord, we become finely attuned to the signs of his presence. The word alerts us to the promise that he will most certainly come; the word encourages us to watch and to wait; and the word assures us that he has come and dwells amongst us. So Advent is a time of pondering the word, allowing it to form us and guide us. Our Advent prayer is that Jesus will truly come, that we will recognise him, and that we will rejoice in the peace he brings.

Prayer

Let us be attentive to the signs of your presence, Lord, so that when you come you will find us ready to greet you and eager to wait on you. In watching for you, we hear the longings of our heart as we look for salvation, knowing that only you can bring us true peace. Help us to be bearers of your promise that, through us, others will hear of your coming and will find hope. We ask this through you, our Lord, for ever and ever. Amen.

When you come, Lord, bring us peace.
When you come, Lord, show us mercy.
When you come, Lord, stay with us.
This day and every day.
Amen.

St Francis Xavier

3 December

Francis was born at the castle of Xavier, near Pamplona in Spain, in 1506. At the age of eighteen he went to study at the University of Paris, where he met St Ignatius Loyola. He was one of the first Jesuits, the popular name for the Society of Jesus founded by St Ignatius. After Francis was ordained priest, Ignatius sent him to India.

In Goa Francis reformed the numerous relaxed Portuguese Catholics who were notorious for their cruelty to slaves, their open concubinage and their neglect of the poor. Francis comforted the sick in hospitals and those in prison, and he offered Mass with lepers every Sunday. To instruct the ignorant and simple he put words of the catechism to popular tunes. For the next seven years he worked in Southern India, in Ceylon, Malacca, the Molucca islands, and the Malay peninsula. He set himself to learn the native language and lived as a native. His food was that of the poorest, rice and water; he slept in a hut, on the ground. So many people were baptised that Francis was so tired he could hardly move his arms.

In 1549 he went to Japan, landing in Kagoshima. Francis set about learning Japanese and he translated a simple account of Christian teaching. After a year he had one hundred converts and the authorities forbade him to preach any more. He moved on to Hirado where he was well received by the ruler and he made more converts in a few weeks than he had made at Kagoshima in a year. When he left Japan the total number of Japanese Christians was about 2,000. Within 60 years they resisted fierce persecution, even to death. In 1552 Francis returned to Goa, but left after a few months to go to China. On the way he fell ill and died on the island of Chang-Chuen-Shan, with only his Chinese companion at his side.

It was the 3rd of December 1551, St Francis was forty-six years old. He was buried the next day in the presence of four people, Antony, a Portuguese and two slaves. The coffin was packed with quicklime in case the remains had to be moved. Eventually the body was taken to

Goa where physicians verified that it was incorrupt, and it became an object of popular pilgrimage. In 1927 Pope Pius XI declared St Francis Xavier as the patron of foreign missions. One of St Francis Xavier's companions described him thus:

He is a true father; no one can see him without great consolation, the very sight of him seems to move to devotion; he is a man of middle height, he always holds his face up, his eyes are full of tears, but his look is bright and joyous, his words few and exciting to devotion. His very look kindles in men an inexpressible desire to serve God.

St Francis' last words were from the Te Deum, "In te, Domine, speravi, non confundar in aeternam" "O Lord, in you have I put my trust, I shall never be confounded."

Thought

To believe is important, and to understand what we believe is important too. Francis Xavier was a wonderful communicator of faith, and his catechesis brought many to fuller, deeper faith. He taught with dedication and with a passion for the things of Christ. We who believe in Christ should always seek to understand what we believe, and to deepen that understanding that we might grow in faith, and help others to grow too. Francis' example is before us, inspiring us.

Prayer

Lord, give us faith that we might believe in you with all our heart, soul, mind and strength. Give us understanding, that we might truly appreciate what we believe. And give us a love for what we believe and understand, that our relationship with you will become stronger and stronger each day. As we imitate Francis, may others see in us an example to follow. We ask this in your name. Amen.

When we find it hard to believe, O God, grant us faith.
When we have doubts, give us courage to face them.
When we feel weak, may our sisters and brothers in faith keep us strong.
Amen.

Christmas Day

25 December

At Midnight Mass the church is filled with light; the priest wears white vestments, the people sing carols. The figure of Jesus, the new-born baby, is put into the manger. Mary and Joseph kneel next to him; the ox and the donkey look on and the shepherds gather round. The birth of this little boy has brought joy and hope to the world, because in him the bright light of God's love overcomes the darkness in people's hearts.

At the first Christmas all the longings of God's faithful people were filled. God came to us as a person we can see. St John says, "he lived among us and we saw his glory, the glory that is his as the only Son of the Father, full of grace and truth."

On 25th December the days in the northern hemisphere have just passed their shortest and at last the nights start to draw out. Before Jesus was born the Romans used to celebrate this time of the year as the time of the Birth of the Unconquered Sun. When the days were darkest, they knew that the sun would return to bring spring and summer. As Christianity spread across the Roman empire in the west the Church gave a new meaning to this time of the year. The sun returns and darkness recedes. Jesus brings a light which never fades, and the darkness can never overcome it. So although we do not know the actual birthday of Jesus, the 25th of December is a very good time to celebrate it.

The Romans also celebrated their festivities with light, fire and food. Evergreens decorated the houses and people gave presents, especially to the poor. A lot of our Christmas customs date from that time, others are more modern. Evergreens are a symbol of eternity. The trees keep their leaves when other trees are bare. Christians used holly because the spines on its leaves remind us of the crown of thorns put on Jesus before he was crucified. The bright red berries are reminders of the blood Jesus shed and so they have become symbols of his love. In Norway and Sweden holly is called the Christ-thorn. Ivy intertwined with holly came to be a symbol of the love between husband and wife. The two joined together represent peace and harmony in the home.

The custom of having Christmas trees is quite recent. Prince Albert, the husband of Queen Victoria, put a tree up at Windsor castle in 1841 and the custom grew very quickly from then on. Christmas cards first appeared in 1843. Sir Henry Cole sent cards to his friends showing pictures of people enjoying a Christmas feast and pictures of food being given to the poor.

Charles Dickens' book A Christmas Carol, has also influenced how we think a 'traditional' Christmas should be. But there is an even older tradition. The first crib came about through St Francis of Assisi in 1223. Francis spoke to the people gathered in the light around the manger about the birth of the Son of God; Jesus the poor king, the little child of Bethlehem. He spoke with such joy that the child Jesus, who had been forgotten by so many, found a place once again in their hearts and minds.

Thought

At the Annunciation, Mary received the promise that she was to bear God's Son. And in the fullness of time, that promise was fulfilled. God was faithful, as God always had been, and always will be. But neither Mary nor the prophets of old could fully understand the gift God was offering at Christmas: the unknowable, unseen God was coming to live amongst people, that they might be saved. Not even a lifetime of pondering could fully reveal this mystery of God's love.

Prayer

Heavenly Father, in your Son Jesus Christ, heaven has come down to earth, that earth may be raised up to heaven. We celebrate his birth as a happy day for ourselves and for the world. Peace has been promised to us, and now is born to us; we need no longer be afraid. May his birth bring us, and all the world, true peace; may we rejoice at his presence amongst us, and take hope in the great news that our God has come close. Through the same Christ our Lord. Amen.

Angels rejoice because the Son of God has been born on earth, bringing peace.
Shepherds rejoice, because the one who is to be called 'Good Shepherd'
*   has come to them*
Wise men rejoice, because Wisdom has come down from on high, and
*   dwells amongst us Amen.*

Notes